PENGUIN

A Hear

RIO HOGARTY has been fostering children – informally and formally – for most of her life. At the 2010 People of the Year Awards she won an award created especially for her, Mother of the Year. She lives with her family in Clondalkin, Dublin.

Megan Day has been a scientific writer for twenty years. After moving from North Carolina to Ireland, she was befriended by the indomitable Rio Hogarty and found, first, a great friend and, second, an amazing story that just had to be written. She lives in County Kildare with a dog and – at the last count – four cats.

PENGUIN BOOKS

A House So Big

A Heart So Big

RIO HOGARTY

with Megan Day

PENGUIN BOOKS

PENGUIN BOOKS

Published by the Penguin Group
Penguin Books Ltd, 80 Strand, London WC2R ORL, England
Penguin Group (USA) Inc., 375 Hudson Street, New York, New York 10014, USA
Penguin Group (Canada), 90 Eglinton Avenue East, Suite 700, Toronto, Ontario, Canada M4P 2Y3
(a division of Pearson Penguin Canada Inc.)
Penguin Ireland, 25 St Stephen's Green, Dublin 2, Ireland (a division of Penguin Books Ltd)
Penguin Group (Australia), 707 Collins Street, Melbourne, Victoria 3008, Australia
(a division of Pearson Australia Group Pty Ltd)
Penguin Books India Pvt Ltd, 11 Community Centre, Panchsheel Park, New Delhi – 110 017, India
Penguin Group (NZ), 67 Apollo Drive, Rosedale, Auckland 0632, New Zealand
(a division of Pearson New Zealand Ltd)
Penguin Books (South Africa) (Pty) Ltd, Block D, Rosebank Office Park,
181 Jan Smuts Avenue, Parktown North, Gauteng 2193, South Africa

Penguin Books Ltd, Registered Offices: 80 Strand, London WC2R ORL, England

www.penguin.com

First published 2014
003

Material from this book was previously published in *Beneath My Wings*

Set in 12.5/14.75pt Garamond MT Std
Typeset by Jouve (UK), Milton Keynes
Printed in Great Britain by Clays Ltd, St Ives plc

A CIP catalogue record for this book is available from the British Library

ISBN: 978–1–844–88324–0

www.greenpenguin.co.uk

MIX
Paper from
responsible sources
FSC
www.fsc.org FSC™ C018179

Penguin Books is committed to a sustainable
future for our business, our readers and our planet.
This book is made from Forest Stewardship
Council™ certified paper.

This book is dedicated to all of the people who have come and gone in my life – big ones, small ones, those who came for a while, and those who came to stay.

I wouldn't have missed a minute of it.

Author's Note

A crucial part of being a foster parent is respecting a child's privacy. It is a lifelong commitment. For this reason I hope you can understand that, while everything told here is true, to protect the privacy of children who have been part of my life (many of them now adults with children of their own), their stories have been broken down and reconstructed. Indeed, many of those who lived with me over the years generously agreed to be featured in the book and said they were happy to be identified. However, rather than apply different approaches to different stories, and for fear of inadvertently including details that would reveal anyone's real circumstances, everyone named in the book – apart from my husband and children (and public figures) – has been given a new name, and identifying information has been changed to a greater or lesser extent.

One day, when I was eleven years old, I brought Mary home with me after school for tea. She stayed for three weeks.

Mary was always a quiet type but you could tell that a lot was going on behind her steady expression. She didn't say much, but had a lot of imagination and loved to read and listen to the radio. Depth was what she had. People would always say that Mary was an example of still waters that ran deep.

We all knew that things weren't great for her at home. Her father was a labourer and was out of work more than he was in it. And her mam was a good Catholic wife. Meaning she was whelping a new brother or sister for Mary just about every year. Number eight had been born just before school started.

I knew Mary was glad to get back to school. Just one more thing that set her apart – she actually liked school. But over the summer something about her had changed. She seemed to be living rougher than usual – clothes a bit more unkempt, the occasional scrape or bruise. Fights with her sisters, she said.

Mind you, I had more bruises and scrapes than anyone I knew – including the boys. In my mind, they were badges of honour, a source of real bragging rights. I had a scar on my left knee that I was extremely proud of, where I had fallen on a plank that had a nail in it. I remember when I stood up, the nail still sticking into my leg, a trickle of blood winding down my shin, that Katie Feeney screamed. It was an absolute high point of my summer.

But for Mary it was different. Some days she just walked a bit gingerly, as if her back hurt. One time, when we were picking blackberries, her sleeve got pushed up and I saw a raw, red mark that completely encircled her arm just above the wrist. She caught me looking at it. Her expression never changed, she just pulled her sleeve back down. I took the hint and didn't ask about it.

A couple of weeks after we had gone back to school, she had a smudge under her eye that she tried to cover with her hair. And I noticed that, for the third day in a row, she had not brought her lunch. As we sat in a circle in the corner of the school hall, the lunchtime noise of a hundred kids burbling around us, I passed her half of my ham sandwich.

I was not unaware that many people had less than my family did. My mother went to great lengths, frequently, to point it out to me, my brother and sisters. It was something I grew up knowing about.

Though the scope of it escaped me, I knew that many of the families around us struggled. It is hard to explain to people now how easily we adapted to poverty back then. It was an element of nature – an inevitability, like rain. None of us had a lot, but many were teetering on a desperate edge.

Mary nibbled her half of the sandwich. She was trying to make it last, stretching out each mouthful, since later it might be only the memory she had to chew on. Before she could finish it, I handed her my apple.

She raised her eyebrows.

'I have two apples today.' It was a lie.

Mary bit into the apple and nodded. She knew I was lying. And she knew why. She didn't make a fuss, just ate the apple and let it go. It's good to have friends like that.

After school, she came to my house and we did the usual mucking about with the gang. The afternoon got very late but she was in no hurry to go home. My mother asked if she would like to stay for tea, so Mary stayed.

After tea, we did our homework together. Well, she did her homework. I was rolling around on the floor playing cars with my baby brother. Mary wrote in her exercise books so neatly and deliberately. And her satchel was in such good order that she could actually find a pencil and a ruler when she needed them. I admit, I was a bit awestruck.

As the evening progressed, I noticed that Mary glanced at the kitchen clock occasionally with a look of dread. She hated seeing the time going by. I don't know how I knew that – at the time she told me nothing directly – but I sensed that she dreaded something. Dreaded leaving us; dreaded going home.

On a whim, I asked my mother if Mary could stay the night and go to school with me in the morning. I had never had a friend over on a school night before. My mother frowned at me, but with Mary hovering over my shoulder, she did not want to appear ungenerous.

'Will it be all right with your mother, Mary?' she asked.

Mary nodded fervently.

And that was it. Over the next few days, between the

two of us, we kept coming up with more excuses as to why she didn't need to go home.

My mother pouted a bit, and I could tell she was put out, but she was too proud to turf Mary out. It was my da who sat down with me one night, while Mary was in the loo, and asked me what was going on.

I told him what little I knew. And it wasn't much.

'Let me look into it.' That was all he said.

It was years later when I learned what had happened. My father knew who Mary's father was, of course, though they did not move in the same circles. But Da, my uncle and one of our neighbours all knew where Mr Farrelly went to drink.

One night, after Mary's da had spent money he didn't have at the pub, the three men were waiting for him. They followed him for a while, then cornered him in a secluded part of a quiet lane. My father spared me the details, but apparently between the three of them they 'explained' to Mr Farrelly what they thought of a man who drank the food money, then beat his wife and children. A few cracked ribs, a broken nose and some loosened teeth apparently convinced him of the error of his ways. Especially when he was reminded that they would be keeping an eye on the family from now on. Mr Farrelly's behaviour improved. Even better, after a couple of months, Mrs Farrelly finally found the strength to pack up her kids and move in with her sister. Mary's father was out of her life for good.

Every once in a while, over the next couple of years, I would have Mary over for tea after school. She would always go straight home afterwards.

PART ONE
A Magical Childhood

Everything about my childhood was special – at least, it seems so, looking back. It has always been a shock to me to find children who don't have magic and adventure, love and security in their lives. It seems to me that those are things every child is entitled to.

I

The year that I turned twenty-five seemed to be a year of babies. It was 1962 and I was already well settled into married life. My husband was a butcher and I ran a small dress shop. My daughter Gwen was toddling around and my son Patrick was just a newborn. And then my dear friend Janet showed up on my doorstep with her announcement.

Janet and I had gone to school together. She had a good job at Arnott's department store and still lived at home. She had never shown much interest in the local lads we knew. Her parents were beginning to think she would never get hitched, and then she delighted them by taking up with a nice-looking English fella who worked at a betting shop. Nigel was his name.

I never liked Nigel. Now, I wouldn't say so then to Janet. She was mad about him and it was her first serious case of love, so I let it be. I figured it would run its course, one way or another.

I had forgotten, obviously, that Nature has a way of making us change course. And Nature had definitely had her way.

'I'm pregnant.' She stared down into her coffee cup, sitting on the other side of my kitchen table. I was giving her a fierce look through my glasses, but she was clever enough to know not to look up.

'Well. Shall we start picking out the wedding invitations?'

She shrugged. 'I suppose so. He hasn't said anything yet.'

'He hasn't said anything?'

'I told him last night. He . . . em . . . wasn't happy.'

'Ah, shit. He didn't hit you or anything, did he?' I was ready to grab a broom handle and give him a talking-to myself, if that was the case.

'No, no. He's nothing like that, Rio. He just got very quiet. When I asked him what we should do, he said he'd have to think about it.'

'What is there to think about?'

'His family back in England, I guess. I don't know.'

'Well, when you see him tonight you'd better explain to him what is expected. He wanted to play house – now he gets to play for keeps.'

'Yeah, he knows. It's just not what we'd planned, ya know?'

I grabbed her hand. 'No, it never is. But plans can change and still work out.'

She smiled.

The next day she was back. I was expecting a bubbly bride-to-be to skip up my stairs. She was stoop-shouldered and her eyes were puffy.

Oh dear.

I set a cup of coffee in front of her on the table. 'So, how's things?'

She sniffed.

Shit.

'Oh, Rio – he didn't answer any of my calls yesterday. I called him at his place and I called him at work.'

'The gobshite. Well, we'll go to his place and roust him.'

Tears were flowing now. 'I went there this afternoon. He's . . . he's . . .'

That did it. Her shoulders started to shake and the tears poured down her cheeks in ribbons of salty grief.

'Oh, Rio – he's gone!'

Double shit.

I threw my arms around her. 'Now, now. He probably just needed to get away for a day or two to figure out how to make this all work. I don't know how it is that men do what they do and then seem absolutely knocked for a loop when they have to face the consequences.'

She was shaking her head. 'No, no. They said he's completely moved out. He told his landlord he was . . . he was . . . going home.' This brought a new eruption of tears.

'Home, as in England? He went back to bloody England?'

She nodded wordlessly.

Triple bloody shit.

I sat next to her and put both my hands on hers. 'Look at me.'

She blinked back the tears and looked up, her lip trembling.

'What do you want to do? Tell me.'

'I – I want to get married and have the baby.'

I nodded. 'Fine. We can do all of that except for the getting-married bit.'

'What?'

'We can't make him come back. He may come back later of his own free will. But in the meantime you need to deal with this, with him or without him. If you want to have this baby, then let's have it.'

'"Let's"?'

'Sure enough. What will your parents say when you tell them?'

'Oh, God. Oh, Rio, I think I'm going to be sick.'

I patted her back. 'No, you're not. We'll face this and we'll make it work.'

She gulped. 'My parents will kill me! And then they'll make me give the baby up. I know they will.'

I decided not to point out that killing her now would remove all need for adoption. 'Okay, so it's best they don't know.'

Now she looked at me as if I'd been sniffing paint-thinner. 'I don't see how on earth they'll *not* know! Hard to miss a big pregnant woman in the house.'

I was running a slew of scenarios through my head. Some were crazy even for me. But I came up with one that I thought, Yes, that might work. It just might work.

'All right now.' I took her hand again. 'This is what we'll do.'

Rio's Single-mother Pregnancy Plan

1. Wear loose clothing. Start now and continue on so that there won't be a sudden change. Make sure that you choose roomy, loose, baggy clothes so that no one can tell how big you are under there. If anyone asks, just say that you like

dressing comfortably and then start discussing your painful menstrual cramps in detail. This is an especially powerful deterrent when used with men and acts as a useful diversion with women.

2. Start eating like there's no tomorrow. Every time your parents and friends see you, they should see you stuffing some fattening food into your mouth. Keep biscuits, chocolate and crisps on hand at all times.

3. When asked why you are eating so much, start to sniffle and moan about something (see point 1 for a possible topic). Having the 'blues' is always considered an appropriate reason for overeating.

Janet was a star student. Her parents never suspected a thing. She was one of those lucky women who gained weight but didn't develop an obviously pregnant shape, so the baggy clothes worked a treat. A couple of other friends and I started wearing baggy jumpers as well. Her parents became resigned to the fact that it was some fashion fad we'd all fallen for. Also, as the months went by, Janet managed to disguise her pregnant-woman waddle.

In her last few weeks, she kept a suitcase packed and hidden under her bed. On the morning when she started having pains, she grabbed the suitcase and told her parents she was going away on a holiday with me for a week or two.

I collected her and took her to the hospital and she had a lovely tiny (but healthy) baby girl. She named her Rose.

We brought Rose to my house. Janet stayed with her for the full two weeks of her 'holiday', then went home. Her parents were delighted that she'd got over the eating binges and started wearing better-fitting clothes again. Obviously the holiday had done her good.

I saw a lot of Janet after that — she was at the house nearly every day and stayed involved in everything her little one did. And she never heard a word from Nigel ever again. It has never ceased to amaze me that there are people in this world who go out and about like nothing has happened and never make any effort to be a part of the life they created.

Rose grew up believing that I was her mother. It was many years later, when she'd finished school and was about to go to university, that we sat down with her and explained that 'Aunt' Janet was really her mother. This may sound like it should have been an astounding bit of information that could do a child's head in. But you need to remember that Rose had grown up in a household in which I had foster children and neighbours' children and friends' children and children I had taken in off the streets coming and going all the time. I wouldn't say she wasn't surprised, but she had been accustomed to the way I dealt with things. She was also old enough to understand how impossible it would have been for her mother to do anything different.

Above and beyond all of that, she knew that Janet had always loved her and always been there for her.

In the end, children generally know what really counts.

2

I am seventy-six years old now, have raised two children of my own and 140-odd others – some for just a few weeks, some for most of their young lives – and sometimes even I have a hard time remembering that I was once a child myself. But, looking back, I know that it was my incredible luck to have a wonderfully happy childhood. It made me believe that every child deserves the same. Whether it was my schoolfriend Mary, or little Rose, daughter of my friend Janet, from very early on I reached out without thinking much about it.

Of course, the funny thing about my happy childhood was that, from the very first day I came into the world, I was not what anyone expected me to be. I was not the son my da had been hoping for as a first-born, while my skinned knees and wild ways meant that I was never the ladylike little girl my mam had wanted.

While their expectations were still intact, my parents had given me a lovely, lyrical name: Rita Mary O'Reilly. Yet even that did not turn out as planned. Before long, my da was calling me Richeen – his little Richeen. Hearing it so often, I came to believe Richeen was my proper name. On my first day at school, when the gaggle of children wanted to know what I was called, I was surprised to find that 'Richeen' did not roll easily off the tongues of five-year-olds.

'Reechy?'

Absolutely not.

'Reetsie?'

'No,' I insisted. 'It's Richeen.'

My new friend Mary was particularly unimpressed. 'I don't like it.' She sniffed. A moment later, she added, 'I like Rio better.'

And I guess I did too, because I have been Rio ever since. Well, I was always Richeen to my da, of course.

Having a different name suited my temperament – which to my da was 'spirited', and to my ma, 'difficult'. In my mind, it was also a name that meant I didn't have to be treated like a girl – or act like one. Tree-climbing, running barefoot through the fields, scaling walls and jumping off them – my mother thought that a girl wearing a skirt wouldn't do such things. She was wrong.

I suppose it caused tension between them, that my da loved my boyish disposition and my mother despaired of it. But it is only now that I realize what must have been the case: at the time, I felt loved by the two most important people in my life, one with complete acceptance, the other with chagrin. But, still, love me they did. And that bed-rock of love was the ground from which I launched myself into one adventure after another. Like a puppy who had never known a collar and leash, I followed my nose and my curiosity wherever they led me.

My grandfather introduced me to the hidden magical world right in my own back garden. He told me all about the faerie folk living in the greenery; I knew of their kingdoms and domains, their music, legendary feasts, and the charms that could beguile humans.

Oh, how I wanted to be beguiled.

We would spend hours exploring the garden for signs of the wee ones, and put our ears to the ground, listening for the tell-tale sounds of their revels. In the early morning, following a rainy night, we would hunt for the rings of rising mushrooms, a sure sign that they had favoured our garden as the location for one of their magical cities.

I never doubted they were there. In many ways, even today, I still do not doubt them.

There was never anything about Nature that frightened or intimidated me, which was not a sign of bravery, more a pig-headed belief in my own immortality.

One winter was abnormally cold so my mother had bought me a lovely new coat, hat and gloves. I was not averse to the idea of looking like a girl – I wore my new attire proudly and was quite delighted with myself. But when Janet, Mary and I were walking across the rectory grounds – a favourite place to play – the frozen fish pond was too fascinating to resist.

Instead of the rippling, slightly scummy surface with the flashes of the darting gold carp below, all we could see was a crusty flatness, dusted with snow.

'Jaysus, the fish must be frozen!' Janet was somewhere between terrified and morbidly fascinated.

'Wouldn't they be able to live under the ice? Couldn't

they keep themselves warm and find things to eat under there?' Mary was always a bit more practical.

'Let's go and see.' That, of course, was me. I was never good with theory.

We walked to the very edge between the frozen grass and the forlorn, stiff reeds that bordered the water. We peered down, fully expecting to see the solid bodies of the goldfish embedded in the ice like pebbles. Instead, we couldn't see much of anything.

I poked my booted foot onto the ice. 'It seems really solid.' As if I knew.

Mary came up with a good plan. 'I bet we could run all the way across.'

Now there was an amazing possibility – running across a pond! My feet tingled at the idea of skimming across the surface where, during the summer, we had thrown bread-crumbs to be gobbled by the overfed goldfish.

'Yes, I think we could!'

'All right, here I go.'

Janet was off, dashing across the ten-foot width of the pond about as quickly as an eight-year-old girl in a bulky coat and boots could go. She got to the other side, turned around and jumped up and down. 'Come on! Come on!'

Then Mary made her mad dash. There was an alarming cracking sound just before she reached the other side, but she was grinning as she bounced up and down next to Janet.

'Come on! Come on!' They were both shouting now.

I started across. Somewhere in the middle, it occurred to me that we had still not solved the puzzle of what had happened to the fish. I stopped and looked down. I could see a difference in the colour of the ice, that there was an edge to the chalky part I was standing on and the darker bit below . . . which was water.

'Hey!' I called. 'There *is* water under there! The fish must be swimming around below the ice!'

I bent over, scanning the watery layers beneath me, looking for a sign of our scaly gold friends.

There was another alarming crack.

'What's that?' Mary looked back towards the rectory. To be fair, we had never stood on ice before. We didn't know what the cracking meant or where it came from.

Then I noticed the marks in the ice. It was as if I was suddenly in the middle of a spider's web constructed from shards of glass. Then the solidity beneath me shifted.

I don't remember making any sound. Janet and Mary insist that I shrieked like a banshee but, then, they would – since they got to stay dry and watch me crash through the ice and plop like a rock to the bottom of the pond.

I suppose it should have been the shock of the cold that got to me, but that's not what I remember. It was the falling . . . down and down until my feet hit the gooey bottom. Instinctively I propelled myself up to the surface.

The water was only barely over my head. Janet and Mary were goggling, like the fish in the pond probably were, when I spluttered to the surface. The ice around me had crackled into smithereens and I was able to work my way over to where the water was shallower.

With my feet firmly planted and my head above water, I walked out of the pond and stood, dripping, next to the girls.

It was suddenly silent – and I realized that Mary and Janet had been screaming at me up until that moment.

'Get out of there, Rio!'

'Don't drown!'

'Come over this way!'

'Your ma is going to kill you!'

In spite of that last sobering remark, as we all stood there, the two of them warm and dry and me dripping, with bits of greenish slime clinging to me, we couldn't help ourselves: we went from giggling to laughing ourselves sick in thirty seconds flat.

All the way home, in spite of my chattering teeth, we laughed and relived the adventure. It became epic in the retelling – an adventure on the Arctic tundra full of frozen treachery.

When I got home, I was still laughing about it and ran in to tell my ma.

'Ma! Ma! Guess what happened!'

Oops. Her icy response was more chilling than my plunge in a frozen carp pond.

All I could think of was the adventure of it, the hilarity, the surprise. All she could see was my new coat, soaked and slimy.

I was stripped out of my freezing wet clothes, a hot bath was prepared, and the new coat, hat and gloves were taken away to be cleaned and dried. I believe they all recovered nicely. But I don't know. The next time I went out, I was given my old coat. I never saw the lovely new one again.

After the frozen-pond incident, my mother made me

promise that my reckless tomboy days were over. She had sensed, as mothers do, that I felt the loss of my lovely new coat rather keenly. This, she assumed, was a sign that I was turning a corner.

For the next couple of weeks I kept my promise. I refused to be drawn into climbing over garden walls if I could walk around them; I resisted crawling on my stomach in the mud even though I knew it would have got me into the best hiding place ever for hide-and-seek; I turned down the dare to see how hard my fountain pen had to be squeezed before the ink would squirt out of the sides instead of the tip (that was a tough one – I was dying to see how it went).

But I had forgotten about the tree. No one could say no to the tree.

Just inside the gate of Kimmage Manor, the Holy Ghost fathers' church and rectory, there was a majestic oak tree that appeared to be about the same age as God. The trunk was as big around as a car and it was nearly as tall as the church spire. Best of all, its limbs were thick, the bottom ones fairly low to the ground, and the progression of their leafy arms staggered upwards in an inviting array somewhere between a ladder and a staircase.

The way the branches bunched together in places, with knobby galls like handholds in between, was a tree-climber's dream. To us, it was as if Jesus had placed the tree on his holy ground as an example of what the perfect climbing tree should be.

The challenge, of course, was how high one could

climb up it. The record was currently held by a boy called Dominic, who had got himself level with the top of the stained-glass window over the church door. Some were convinced that this record would never be broken.

You see, it was not just a matter of climbing the tree. Given its symmetry, that was easy. The problem was the priests. Knowing an irresistible temptation when they saw one, they had strictly forbidden us to climb it. Which had exactly the effect you would expect: we had devised ways of climbing it when they weren't looking.

The trick was for a few of us to gather under the tree with our schoolbags and to sit on the grass, under the leafy boughs, with books in hand as if we were studying. The kids with the books were the lookouts. While one intrepid climber began their ascent, the ones with the books had the job of shouting a signal when a priest came into view. The usual alarm was to yell, 'Look at this!' while pointing at something in a book. Whoever was up in the tree would know to come to a complete stop and not draw attention to themselves. When the priest had gone, the all-clear was called and climbing could continue.

The Great Tree Climbing Challenge was not planned. Like many pivotal moments in life, it was completely spontaneous. On an unusually mild day in late winter, a gang of us were walking past the tree when the gauntlet was thrown down. Perhaps it was a blessing, perhaps it was a curse, but I was a great tree-climber. I found shifting myself from branch to branch almost as effortless as walking – Janet rather dismissively accused me of being part monkey. Regardless of whether it was a good thing or not, it was a talent. And when Brian O'Donnelly told me that no one would ever climb higher than Dominic, I couldn't let it stand. Not so much because of my ego but because it was simply untrue. I knew I could climb all the way to the very top of that tree. So, with lookouts in place, books in their hands, I started my climb.

The first leg was the only part that could not be climbed alone. The lowest branch was just out of my reach so Brian and Mary stood on some stacked schoolbags and hoisted me with linked hands to my launching point for the big climb.

Hand over hand, swinging one leg at a time over tree limb after tree limb, I was doing well. I had just reached the particularly large, broad branch that was always the first stopping point when I heard the alarm. I scooted as close as I could to the trunk and held my breath.

My enforced rest was short – it was just a priest hurrying past. Within moments I was back on the climb.

I'm not fearful of heights, but I have a healthy respect for gravity. I knew that looking down could make me dizzy so I kept my head up, and continued to climb and climb. Shouts of encouragement floated up on occasion, and a few hoots that were meant to distract me – apparently Dominic had arrived and wanted to make sure his record was secure.

I had a couple of minor close calls – scraped my knee, grazed my knuckles, got smacked across the eyes by a whippy branch – but I slogged on, always looking above me, always searching for that next handhold.

As I pulled myself up onto one particularly knobbly

branch I heard a commotion from below. It wasn't the usual alarm.

'Take a look from where you are!' It was Mary.

Then I heard other voices: 'It's the window! It's the window!'

I looked towards the front of the church and, sure enough, I was level with the stained-glass window. I was almost to the high mark that Dominic had set.

I looked down for a moment to wave to them.

Whoa.

I started to sway a little bit as the shock of their seemingly tiny faces hit me. I turned away to look at the stained glass again. That was better.

A bit shaken, but no less determined, I reached above me to a medium-sized branch that could propel me, if I swung on it slightly, to a bigger branch a bit higher and to the right of the branch I was on. I had just started the swing when I heard the alarm.

'Look at this!' wafted up to me in a high-pitched chorus that sounded more urgent than usual.

I flailed my legs towards the bigger branch, but it was slick with dead leaves and I got no footing. Instead I swung back and forth, finally coming to a halt with nothing beneath my feet at all. I hung there motionless, knowing I mustn't make any sound or movement that would cause a priest to look up.

I waited for the all-clear, picturing the priest scurrying past the gate, oblivious to the anxious children with their upside-down school books. As soon as he was gone, I would get the signal.

So I waited.

My arms started to tremble. I didn't want to swing again towards the branch – it might make too much noise. Or the movement might catch someone's eye. Feeling my fingers getting slippery, I dug the toes of my shoes into the bark of the tree trunk, trying to take some weight off my arms. That helped for a few minutes.

Still no all-clear. Now my legs and my arms were shaking. What on earth was going on down there?

I managed to get one hand loose and grabbed on to a thicker branch to my left, heading back to the hefty limb I had been standing on before. I seized hold of it and tried to swing my leg over the bigger branch. My leg got over and the small branch slipped from my hand, throwing me off balance. With one leg over the big limb and one hand still on the larger branch, I managed to slip around and end up hanging nearly upside-down, one arm and leg flapping uselessly among the dead leaves. A tiny loose twig fluttered to the ground.

I gasped and turned my attention to the wavering earth below me, expecting to see the accusing glare of a priest blazing back.

But there was no priest. That was good.

But there was also no one else. Everyone was gone – not even a schoolbag in sight.

Hell's bells.

As I wobbled in the air, trying to make sense of my situation, the colours of the stained-glass window to my right caught my eye. I was so close. And I knew that there was a lovely set of branches above my head leading like a staircase to well above the apex of the window.

I was going to do this. At least I didn't have to worry about making a noise. Off I went, swinging myself upright and hoisting myself to the next set of branches, scrabbling up the shallow ledges of ancient grooves and folds in the bark of the tree trunk. My hair got caught on one particularly spindly branch, and as I pushed myself past it, a clump of curls stuck, waving in the puffs of breeze.

Onward and upward, with no looking down and no niggling worries about holes torn in the knees of my stockings, I kept climbing.

The air around me suddenly seemed quite still, the creaking of the branches the only thing I could hear. And then I saw there were no more branches above me big enough to climb on. The next six feet or so tapered off over my head, clumps of dead leaves hanging on tenaciously to thin wispy branches.

As far as climbing went, I had reached the top. I looked out around me – I could see into the opening in the spire where the bell hung. All my life I had heard that bell ring, on Sundays, on holy days, for weddings, funerals and christenings – but I had never seen it. It had bird droppings on it.

It now dawned on me that, at the pinnacle of my tree-climbing career, no one was there to see me. And no one – especially Dominic – would ever believe what I had done.

I sat in a very unladylike way on the last branch that would support me and searched through my coat pockets. Among the used bus tickets, sweet wrappers and petrified chewing gum, I managed to find a bottle cap. I applied the sharp edge to the bark and scraped some shallow markings that looked more or less like an 'R' and an 'O'. Rio O'Reilly had been here.

I spat on my fingers and wiped the initials clean. There.

Now it was time for the descent. For the first time since I had reached the top, I looked straight down.

Double hell's bells.

I had to close my eyes and hold onto the trunk very tightly for a few seconds. After that, I would only look down as far as my next foothold. This was no time to get dizzy.

The climb down took nearly as long as the climb up. Without my lookouts below, I hesitated to go too fast or make too much noise.

At last I made it to the lowest branch. There wasn't a sinner around. I was now cold, hungry and tired, and I had to find a way to get down by myself. After what I had just done, it wasn't an unreasonable challenge.

I tried some exploratory scraping with my foot to see if the bark might be uneven enough to give me a foothold. It was a bit dodgy – slippery in some places, rough and creased in others: it might provide some traction.

I decided to risk it and slipped off the branch, hanging by my hands, scrabbling with my feet until I was stuck in. Now I had to see if there were any small branches or large bumps where I could get a handhold.

'What are you doing there?'

I nearly jumped out of my skin.

The voice was behind me. There was no mistaking Father O'Dowd.

'I sent all you children off half an hour ago. Now get down off that tree.'

I was hanging slightly above his head. It was not clear to me how he expected me to cover the distance. Perhaps he thought I would sprout wings and flutter down in an angelic cloud. I panicked and tried to grab the trunk with my hands, keeping my toes dug in.

I smacked the bottom of my chin squarely on the branch, then fell and landed bumpily near Father O'Dowd's feet, wheezing from having the wind knocked out of me.

He reached down and pulled me upright. I gulped as I felt a trickle from my chin down my neck. I swiped at it with my sleeve.

'You're all right now, aren't you?' Father O'Dowd looked at me with an expression that dared me to say otherwise.

I nodded, not sure what might come out of my mouth. A scream seemed to have curled up on my tongue and was waiting to jump out. I didn't dare give it a chance.

Without another word, I ran off – leaving Father O'Dowd and my initials behind.

It wasn't until years later, when Kimmage Manor was being redeveloped, that the tree was cut down. I could have proved to my friends then, once and for all, that I had reached the top. But, of course, no one was around who might have cared.

My mother knew I had climbed it, though. Well, she knew I had done something. The torn stockings, scraped knuckles, scratched face and filthy shoes were pretty damning evidence. The kind I could usually explain away. But there was no getting around the skin scraped off my chin.

Throughout my entire childhood, it seemed that everyone in the neighbourhood helped at the Holy Ghost fathers' farm. My grandfather worked there several mornings a week and all of us children helped over the summer. There was certainly loads to do. At one time the priests and brothers had been completely self-sufficient – they grew wheat, they raised dairy and beef cattle, they kept poultry, pigs, ducks and sheep. There were also large vegetable and herb gardens. But most of the brothers had become more interested in teaching, and the priests were mostly motivated by fundraising for the church, so it was left to the parishioners to contribute to the farm work. When my granddad went there, I loved to tag along.

My tree-climbing pals, Dominic and Brian, were there a lot. Sometimes they were with their parents. Often they had been assigned farm chores as either a penance or a punishment for some transgression at school. Hard work in the open air was supposed to cleanse them of their ill-begotten ways. Mostly it just cleansed them of whatever common sense they might have had.

To be fair, the farm was a paradise of play for a kid. The big stacks of hay, the huge barns full of nooks and crannies, the wide-open fields, the small sheds crammed with all kinds of weird and interesting objects. We had a fantastic time building forts and castles from hay bales, climbing up ladders, sliding down ropes. It was hard to concentrate on things like chores.

One afternoon I was playing in the piles of hay while my granddad was helping to separate the ewes from the rams. Dominic was supposed to be mucking out the pens where Brother Nolan's prized hens were kept. He still had his shovel in his hand, but was using it to help me rearrange the bales into a stairway so that I could climb up to the edge of the loft without having to use the ladder.

We were pushing a tricky one into place when Brother Nolan came in.

'Dominic!' he roared.

Dominic turned towards him and dropped his shovel.

Brother Nolan looked slightly unhinged at the best of times. Today his frog-like eyes were fairly popping and blue lines throbbed on his temples.

Dominic clumsily retrieved his shovel. 'Sorry, sir. I was just . . . er, I was . . . I was helping Rio.'

Brother Nolan was having none of it. He grabbed Dominic by an ear and twisted. 'You get into that pen and you finish the job now!' With that, he pushed Dominic towards the yard, forcing the shovel into his hand as he did so. Dominic stumbled out, one hand dragging the shovel, the other clapped over his ear.

Brother Nolan paid no attention to me. He just turned on his heel and stormed off. I don't know what made me do it but I picked up a clod of muck and hurled it at his retreating back.

It was my bad luck to have such excellent aim. The dirt

exploded all over his cassock, destroying its pristine black-ness. He wheeled around frighteningly fast – years of being pelted by schoolboys with spit balls, I suppose – and caught me gawping at him like a landed guppy.

'You come here this instant, young lady!'

I licked my lips and looked around for alternatives. I turned and high-tailed it up the stacks of hay and leaped onto the lip of the overhanging loft. I didn't turn to look but I could hear him following. Once in the loft, I zig-zagged around barrels, bags and more bales, and headed for the exit. Not the ladder, mind you. Brother Nolan would only follow me down and eventually his superior size would win the day (at the expense of my ears).

Luckily, there was another way out, one in which my size would be an advantage – the hay chute. This led dir-ectly down into the pens below, where the cows would normally be placidly chewing the cud in colder weather. Today there would be nothing but a hay rack and some squishy piles of cow dung. Well, it would be a soft landing. I lunged for the opening, which was just wide enough for my shoulders, and I plummeted down, landing on my bot-tom in a mixture of mouldy hay and manure.

I heard a yelp above me, which was Brother Nolan real-izing where I had gone. I heard a thud and then ... nothing. Until the yelling started.

I looked up and there were Brother Nolan's feet, sus-pended in the air above me. They were twisting frantically and bits of hay and dirt were drifting down, dislodged by his panicked contortions. The sound was muffled and I couldn't hear his words but I suspected that Brother Nolan was going to have to say a lot of Hail Marys.

I got up and headed for the farmyard. I found Dominic and Brian there, in the special pen for the black and white speckled hens, both shovelling piles of chicken shit into a wheelbarrow. Dominic kept his eyes on the ground and occasionally I heard him sniffle.

'I'm just hiding here for a minute,' I said.

Brian grinned. 'From who?'

'Brother Nolan. He's stuck in the hay chute.'

The boys had a right laugh at that, but then Dominic's face clouded. 'He's going to be in an even worse temper when he gets free.'

'Someone needs to tell him to be nicer,' I said. 'He's just a big bully.'

'Well, no one's going to do that,' Dominic said. 'No one cares what the brothers do to us kids.'

'Someone should.'

We looked at each other for a moment. In the quiet, we could hear the hens clucking inside their neat shed, where they were enclosed while their yard was being cleaned.

'Lads,' I said. 'I have an idea.'

Apart from the ordinary run-of-the-mill variety, Brother Nolan had four prized chickens – Dora, Flora, Carmen and Vivienne. They were French Mottled Houdans. Their white plumage was speckled with black and white spots and they had impressive flouncy crests on their heads. They were indeed lovely.

The master-plan I had come up with was to take the chickens hostage for a few days, just to teach Brother Nolan a lesson. So far all had gone well. We were out in the woods at the back of the farm – Brian, Dominic, Dominic's little sister Tess and me – each of us tying a piece of string to a chicken's legs. The other ends of the strings were tied to a tree. I pulled a handful of corn out of my pocket and scattered it on the ground. The chickens started to peck, occasionally twitching the leg that had the string attached to it, as if it were a bracelet that didn't fit properly. None seemed too interested in seeing how far they could get from the tree – or the corn.

'They seem happy, don't they?' Tess wasn't sure how to tell if chickens were happy, but she thought that quietly pecking at the ground might be a positive hint. Her little hands had shaken when the boys gave her a writhing burlap feed sack to carry to the woods. But scratching feet and sharp beaks aside, she had wanted to help her big brother.

Brian pulled a small tin bowl and a bottle of water out of his bag. I knelt and cleared a spot where the chickens would be able to reach the bowl – and hopefully not knock it over with their strings. But they might: chickens were pretty stupid. We would need to come out here often and make sure the water dish was kept full.

The next part of the plan was to put the feed sacks back where we had found them. I'd thought about that part – if the sacks were missing, everyone at the farm would know it was an 'inside job'. If Brother Nolan was to be properly chastised for his ill-treatment of Dominic and the other boys, he had to fear more than just the petty pranks of the kids who helped at the farm: he had to fear punishment that could come from anywhere at any time. He had to fear the very hand of God.

Once we got back to the periphery of the farmyard, we stopped, hidden behind the prickly hedge. We peered through the foliage and made sure the place was empty. It was dusk, nearly dark, and everything was silent except for the shuffling and snorting of the pigs and cows in the barn on the opposite side of the yard. Someone had to be brave enough to break cover and complete the mission. Brian volunteered. We held our breath for the two minutes it took him to toss the sacks into the shed and race back.

'We'll have to take the long way home,' I said, 'so they won't see us coming from here. They can't know we were anywhere near the chickens today.'

As we made our way back through the woods, Tess couldn't help but wonder if it was a mortal or a venial sin to steal someone's prize chickens. I had explained that we weren't really stealing, just 'borrowing' – without permission – to teach Brother Nolan a lesson. Tess hadn't learned all of her catechism yet but she feared she was on shaky moral ground, no matter how much Brother Nolan needed a lesson.

Suddenly, out of nowhere, a blaze of light burst into our faces and paralysed us.

'Children? What are you doing here at this time of night?'

It was Father O'Dowd. There was no mistaking that

voice. As he towered over us, we gazed up into his face, subsumed in a silence that seemed to throb with guilt.

'Well? What are you children doing out this way at this time of the night?'

My normally glib tongue was stuck in my mouth, like a swollen melon.

Shockingly, it was Tess who spoke up. Tiny Tess with her trembling voice, teardrops edging her wispy eyelashes. 'Oh, Father – we were just at the chapel.'

My head nearly snapped off my neck as I swung around to look at her. Brilliant, I thought – and why did I not think of it?

'The chapel? Whatever would you four need to be going to chapel for at this time of night?'

Instead of a credible, if somewhat cheesy, story escaping her tender lips, Tess broke into a near hysterical sob, crushed under the weight of Catholic guilt. 'Oh, Father! We've done something terrible.'

A thunderous silence followed.

'What exactly is this terrible thing?' Father O'Dowd's voice had that quiet quality that the voices of people with ferocious tempers often display.

Once again, I found my tongue frozen and lumpish. And so, once again, it was Tess who spoke up.

'None of us had been to confession this week, Father. We're taking the long way home as a penance.'

The flashlight flickered across our faces. Truly, we must have looked like the most pathetically guilty little bunch he had ever seen.

'All right, then. It's getting late and your parents will be worried. Off you go.'

It was a miracle.

The next morning, Brother Nolan discovered his chickens were missing and raised the alarm all over the parish. His hysteria was frightening – and very satisfactory.

We dutifully helped to comb the area near the farm, and Brother Nolan was touched to notice that – in our concern – we volunteered to scour the distant woods as well. Although we had to report to him that we had found nothing.

Brother Nolan was heartbroken and prickly with anger as all the searching produced no sign of his prized flock. It was therefore quite baffling when, two mornings after they had disappeared, as he made his usual rounds to collect the average eggs that had been laid by the average hens, he heard some heart-stopping familiar cackling. And there they were – Dora, Flora, Carmen and Vivienne – promenading in their enclosure, as haughty and bright-eyed as the day they had left.

No one ever came forward with a logical explanation for what had happened. It remained a mystery. But the incident had the desired effect: something in Brother Nolan's nature shifted. Perhaps he had some inkling that the Lord was not entirely pleased with him and had sent this trial in order that he might examine his relationship with his flock – the non-feathered kind. He actually became a slightly kinder man.

A few days after all the excitement had blown over, I was walking to the farm with Granddad. 'Funny thing,' he said. 'No one remarked on it, but I couldn't help noticing that there were some chicken feathers in a couple of the feed sacks. White feathers, with black spots.'

I said nothing and looked away in case the innocence had slipped off my face. We continued walking, neither of us speaking.

Granddad never mentioned it again. But he smiled whenever he saw those lovely, arrogant hens parading in their special chicken yard.

4

The end of the summer meant blackberries. Gangs of us would go out, with baskets and pillow cases, to collect whatever we couldn't eat from the masses of bushes that grew all around the edges of the fields. We were in the city, but the semi-wild fields crouched around us, like sleeping cats, knowing their days were numbered.

One day I was out with my usual crowd to pick berries. I had reached the ripe old age of ten so most of them were younger than me and needed a bit of minding. One fellow, Derek, still had a hard time distinguishing ripe berries from green ones. He didn't think colour should be the deciding factor. In his mind, if he could reach it, then it was a berry that should be picked. And eaten. He even ate one that had a caterpillar on it. He cried but was unable somehow to spit it out. Derek grew to be a strapping fellow. I think he may owe it all to the caterpillar.

Little Tess was constantly getting snagged by the blackberry briars. Sometimes it was her hair, and she would shriek. Sometimes it was her clothes, and she would cry. Whenever she got a scratch on her hand, it was a major catastrophe with shrieking *and* crying, and all berry-picking had to stop while I attended to her wounds.

Mary, Janet and Nan, Tess's older sister and my friend, were under strict orders from their mothers to bring home enough berries to make a pie. Unfortunately, none of them was clear on exactly how many berries that might be. Janet had a theory she was trying out that meant for every berry she ate she should put two in the basket. As the morning went on, that seemed lopsided and she opted for a one-to-one ratio.

It was warm that day, but not hot, so it did not seem odd to see a fellow in a raincoat approaching. We all noticed him, as he followed the hedge from the far side of the field over to where we were. I couldn't say I knew him, but he looked a bit familiar. As if he bore a resemblance to someone I knew.

The first thing about him that was wrong was that he was so much older than us. Berry-picking was a task for kids and he didn't even have a basket. When I mentioned this, Mary suggested that his coat pockets would probably suffice. If that was the case, he certainly wasn't planning on making a pie.

We carried on with our picking. Tess got caught among some nettles. This created a whole new level of panic, so heightened it actually prevented her from shrieking. It required careful manoeuvring just the same to extricate her stinging ankle without getting her snagged by either more nettles or some briars. By the time I got her loose, my left hand was on fire with nettle stings, and a briar had scratched me just below my eye.

So there we were, Tess freed and only whimpering, Derek making headway with some berries that were only slightly tinged with green, the other girls accumulating enough uneaten berries to make a substantial pie, and me rubbing grass into the nettle-inflamed area of my hand – when we heard the footsteps behind us.

Out of the corner of my eye, I saw the quizzical look on Mary's ever so logical face. I turned and saw our visitor. The man in the raincoat. At the time, I thought he was ancient – at least twenty-two. In my mind, the difference between twenty-two and eighty-seven was rather indistinct. At any rate, he was not one of us and not someone I knew. I wasn't frightened, just curious.

At first he just stood there. The kids continued picking berries. Our visitor seemed unsure what to do next. He was fumbling strangely with both hands in his raincoat pockets. Between the tops of his unlaced boots and the hem of his poorly fitting coat, I caught a glimpse of hairy leg.

My first thought was, Everyone knows you should have your legs covered when you go blackberry picking! For a moment I pictured him shrieking like Tess when he walked into the nettle patch. I was about to point out to him that he might want to reconsider his attire, but something in his oddly attentive gaze distracted me. Maybe I could work my excellent wardrobe advice into a conversation. So I started with 'Hi there. How ya doin'?'

This usually worked a treat in any schoolyard situation. But he just continued fumbling in his pockets and staring at us in what I now noticed was an unblinking and unfriendly kind of way.

At any rate, he had a totally unique ice-breaker of his own. Without having spoken a word to us, he simply pulled the edges of his raincoat apart and stood there – naked as the day he was born. Except for the boots, I guess.

I didn't know a lot about adult male anatomy, but I had changed my baby brother's nappies a time or two. I knew the basics of what we were dealing with. But there was something alien and frightening about the size and insistence of it. I didn't know what it was for, but I knew that this was horribly wrong.

The children all screamed. Baskets and bags were dropped. Our visitor took a menacing step forward. Any doubts I had were dissolved in that instant. I spread my arms out and stood in front of the children. '*Get away from us!*'

I had never shouted so loudly before. I had hoped I could summon enough power through my voice to knock him off his bandy, hairy legs.

He stayed on his booted feet, but seemed to sway a little. And he blinked.

As if on cue, the rest of the gang started screaming and clung together behind me.

'*You go away from us now!*'

The combined momentum of my shouting and their screaming seemed to push him to his tipping point. He pulled the edges of his coat together and backed away. As we continued screaming, he continued shuffling backwards until he finally turned himself around and fell into a stumbling run across the lumpy surface of the field. He disappeared around a hedge.

Small hands grabbed me around my waist and I felt Tess trembling with sobs. The older girls were pale and confused. Derek said, 'What was that?' I didn't know how to answer him.

I said nothing to my parents that evening. I don't know why, but it just seemed like such a personal event, and since the fella had run off, it didn't seem like there was anything left to do. But Janet, Tess and Derek had told their parents, and the next thing I knew my parents had me seated at the kitchen table and were looking at me worriedly.

They asked if it was true that I had chased off a fella in a raincoat. I gave them what details I could, and Da nodded. He looked at my mother. 'I believe that's Mr O'Hara's nephew.'

She gasped a little bit and put a hand to her mouth. Shocking to hear that such things can be done by people you know, I suppose.

Da looked at me. 'He's a bit simple. I'm afraid they've let him run about, thinking he was harmless.'

'Well, he didn't hurt anyone. Not really.'

I don't know how I ended up defending the poor boy, but I admit, I did not do it whole-heartedly. I was years away from understanding what had happened that day, but somehow I knew that some invisible border had been crossed – some razor-thin line between innocence and its loss had been bridged. And for ever after I would have to be dragged across that bridge kicking and screaming.

It was easier for me to understand the love that the O'Hara boy's parents had for their disturbed child than it ever was for me to understand the adults I came across later who seemed incapable of loving their children. My own happy, secure, if somewhat eccentric childhood had left me unprepared for a world in which a child could be unloved, unwanted and uncared-for. Even when such situations were staring me in the face, I always believed that these were temporary lapses brought on by circumstance.

For the most part, I still try to believe that.

5

I enjoyed being a child, but growing up was fun for my two sisters and me, too. I might have started out as a tomboy, but I also liked all the dressing-up, the lipstick, the nylons and high heels, the parties and dancing and, of course, boys.

What a nightmare for my parents – three girls in various stages of hormonal surges. My da instituted some very strict rules to keep us in line. We had to be home by twelve sharp. No ifs, ands or buts, no excuses, no sob stories, and all hell to pay if the curfew was violated. Cinderella never faced such a dire fate when the clock struck midnight. This was meant to be an obstacle to our misbehaving. I saw it more as a challenge.

And I had a partner in crime. After I'd finished climbing trees and tying up chickens, and before I got married, I became good friends with a girl my own age named Doris, who was a great singer and dancer, and a load of laughs. Dancing was the main way we entertained ourselves in those days – and it was also the best way to meet fellas. The favourite dance hall at the time on the south side of the city was the Olympia. I had spent my younger years with skinned knees, running wild, but I had also learned the things girls needed to know – including dancing. So it became a thing for Doris and me on Saturday nights to put on our nylons and lipstick and head to the Olympia.

Doris had a fair-haired beauty and an easy smile – the boys flocked around her. I was more of the dark-haired, well-cushioned sort – but I was never afraid to talk to anyone, could enjoy a pint or two, without getting stupid, and dance all night. So in our own ways, we each had our appeal.

One of my first conquests was a good-looking young fella named Tommy Ferguson. He was nineteen, tall and slender, with brown wavy hair and a dimple when he smiled. Light on his feet, he was one of the best dancers at the Olympia. The other great dancer was his identical twin brother.

Yes, Tommy and Timmy, the Ferguson twins. What a pair. It was like two scoops of your favourite ice cream in one cone. And I was never one to say no to dessert.

Tommy was the first to ask me out. We went to see a film one Friday evening, then for a coffee. I was home by twelve and kept my parents happy by meeting my curfew … and then, when all was quiet, I was out of my ground-floor bedroom window and off with Tommy again to go dancing till *very* late.

I liked Tommy a lot – he was great fun – but I wasn't interested in settling down with something like a boyfriend. Not *one* boyfriend, anyway. One Saturday at the Olympia, Tommy wasn't there – but Timmy was. And, wouldn't you know it?, *he* asked me out for the following Thursday! Lovely.

So we went to a film. And then out for a coffee. I was

home for my curfew . . . then, whoosh, out of the window again and we were off to a dance somewhere. Well, they were *twins*, so the dates were not surprisingly different.

I had a lovely time with each of them. Doris asked which I liked better – which seemed to suggest that I was supposed to choose one. That seemed highly unfair to me. I liked them both – why not have both? I started a juggling act that Barnum and Bailey would have envied. Tommy might call and ask me to go out on Wednesday, and then Timmy might call and ask me out for Thursday. I would generally try to find out where the other one was going to be on a given night so that I could make sure my date and I were on the other side of town.

Sometimes my plans got so convoluted that I could hardly keep them straight – was it Tuesday with Timmy or Thursday with Tommy? Finally, one week, I decided to get back out on the playing field and spend my Saturday night with Doris and the gang at the Olympia. Tommy had phoned and asked me to go to a film: I told him I had to babysit. He said he would play cards with his mates. Timmy had phoned and wanted to hear some music somewhere: I told him I was coming down with a cold, so he said he would go on his own and meet up with some of his friends there.

With the coast clear, I slapped on some lippy and met up with Doris at the dance hall. Things were busy and the music was great – I had just finished a fabulous spin around the dance floor with a nice fella from Crumlin when I felt a tap on my shoulder. I turned around and was shocked to see Tommy – or maybe Timmy – standing there.

'Hiya, darling.' He was grinning. Tommy, I was pretty sure. 'Didn't have to babysit after all? You shoulda phoned me!'

Oops. To which twin had I given that excuse? I had no idea. 'It was very last minute,' I said. I looked over Tommy's shoulder to see the fella from Crumlin give me an odd look, then walk away and start talking to another girl. Damn it.

I looked desperately for Doris to see if I could give her the signal that meant 'Bail me out.' No sign of her.

Tommy put his hands on my waist. 'Well, since we're both here now, let's get out there and have some fun.'

'Er ... yeah. Well, just a minute. Need to catch my breath.' I was scanning the crowd for Doris desperately now.

Then I felt a tap on my shoulder. At last! Reprieve! I turned around with a big smile on my face, expecting to see my pal. No such luck.

'What the hell is going on here?' It was Timmy. Or maybe Tommy. The other, at any rate.

Now it was Tommy's turn. 'What does it look like? Me and Rio are about to dance.'

'Yeah?' Timmy (or Tommy) grabbed my arm. 'I thought you had a cold and couldn't go out tonight? Why would you be too sick to go out with me but well enough to go out dancing?'

Tommy (or Timmy) pulled on my other arm. 'What are you on about? Go out with you?'

'Yeah, we were goin' somewhere. What's it to ya?'

The conversation was getting louder and going on over my head, back and forth, as if I wasn't there. Not being there seemed like a good idea. I tried to wriggle free. Timmy let go, Tommy held on tighter. Or vice versa.

'She was supposed to babysit tonight, otherwise she was goin' out with me!'

'What? You're a liar!'

'No, *you*'re the bloody liar.'

It was getting messy. Though, interestingly, in the light of brotherly competition, neither of them seemed to have considered the lying I had obviously been doing. Thank goodness.

I wriggled my arm free and stepped out of the way. This seemed to be the signal they had been waiting for. Now they could start pummelling the bejesus out of each other, free and clear. I stood still for a moment, partly in shock but also just a wee bit delighted that I had two lads fighting over me. How exciting! Some of the other fellas there jumped in and tried to prise the pair of them apart. As I stood there, gaping, I felt yet another tap on my shoulder.

I turned, and this time it *was* Doris.

'Hell's bells, you'd best get outta here.'

She hauled me out to the front and we sat on the steps and waited for the noise to die down. Doris lit a cigarette and eyed me appraisingly. 'Well, aren't you the little heart-breaker?'

'Ah, bloody hell, I never meant it to turn out like that.' Guilt was starting to rear its ugly head at me. Just a bit. 'I feel terrible. No more twins for me. Bloody not worth it.'

Doris exhaled a long stream of smoke and watched it thoughtfully as it curled into the cold evening air. 'Oh, I don't know.' She took another pull. 'They're pretty cute.'

She looked down at me. 'And they're available again, yeah?'

'You've got to be joking.'

She shrugged and smiled. No, she was definitely not joking. Cheeky!

As is always the case when you're young, those free and easy times were too short. Doris never got serious about either of the Fergusons, but she was pursued, very insistently, by a slightly older fella named Damien, who actually had a job. That was enough, in those days, to practically make a fella a superstar. And he had a good job, too, selling feed and fertilizer to farmers so he travelled a lot. In what seemed to me to be a total lapse in her usual good sense, Doris let herself be swept away – and in a blink they were married. They settled into a little house in Lucan, and before I knew what was what, she was pregnant – with twins!

It seemed like a virus after that. Everyone we knew – including the Fergusons – was getting married. My circle of Saturday-night dance partners was narrowing by the week. Then one night at the Olympia I met someone new, a nattily dressed fella with wavy gingery hair who seemed different from everyone else. He was a bit more serious, yet still liked to have fun. He had a good job as a butcher, right there in the city. And he took to me straight away. His name was Hughie Hogarty.

44

We took up together as dance partners, then started seeing each other during the week for films and music sessions and what-have-you. He was a singer, so we found ourselves with plenty in common, sharing a lot of the same interests and pastimes. What can I say? One thing led to another, and the next thing I knew, I was struck down by the same affliction that had stolen away Doris and so many of my other friends.

Hughie had a sister, Betty, who was a talented seamstress – she made me a wedding dress and, at the age of twenty-two, I marched down the aisle and my father gave me away. I'm not sure which of us cried the most.

And that was it. In a flurry of lace and flowers, I had surrendered to the current that was carrying us all forward, away from the known shores of our younger selves and into some unexplored territory where the footing was less certain. Both the girl with the scabby knees and fearless heart and the teenager with the easy smile and cheeky humour were in some small way diminished.

Now I was Rio Hogarty.

Hughie continued with his job at the butcher's, while Betty and I set up a dress shop, called Michel's. I had trained as a window-dresser right after school, so with my eye for display and Betty's sewing talents, we did well. And, Nature being what it is, it wasn't too long before I was the mother of a baby girl. Not that motherhood slowed me down much.

Doris had her hands full with her twin boys. Her husband seemed always to be away, and week after week she was a bit short on her housekeeping money. I asked her to come in and help me at the shop whenever she could – she could drive the van or stock shelves.

The income from Michel's was good, but not great, and we were always on the lookout to stretch our shillings. It wasn't long before we got into a routine of going to the Dandelion Market on Saturday and Sunday mornings. The square would be a hodgepodge of stalls and tables, with some folks selling things from the boot of their car or the back of their van or truck, with everything you could think of (and a lot you wouldn't have dreamed of) on offer. We loved prowling through the stacks and boxes, hunting for the best bargains on household items, like laundry soap and toilet paper. We got to know the traders and the other regular customers well and enjoyed the company and the banter as much as the shopping.

Doris's husband had a good job, so I could never understand why she always seemed to be struggling for cash. I knew she had more expenses than I did, what with her having two children while I only had the one, but it still seemed as if Damien was deliberately going off to his job 'on the road' and leaving her short of money every week. Those business trips of his seemed to keep him away longer and longer. Fortunately, Doris had her mother nearby to help her with the boys, but even so the strain of it was getting to her, I could tell.

Then one day Damien went off to work and never came back. There was no word from him. Days went by, and Doris waited. Then it was a week. The week turned into several weeks. She phoned him at work and was fobbed off by various people, saying he was out on the road and couldn't get in touch with her, but not to worry, they were sure he was fine.

But there was no money coming in.

On a morning about six weeks after Damien had disappeared, I was behind the counter at Michel's when the shop door flew open and Doris burst in, a newspaper in her hand.

'That stupid, double-timing, bloody cheating liar!' she shouted, waving the newspaper and then throwing it onto the counter in front of me.

Thank goodness there were no customers in the shop at the time. I saw the curtain to the back room twitch a little and Betty peeped out, looking completely terrified. She saw it was Doris, realized it was probably perfectly logical to be terrified, and let the curtain fall back.

'Jesus, Doris, what's this all about? You look like you could eat the face off someone.'

She slapped her hand on the newspaper. 'Look at it! Page seven. Just bloody look at it.' She folded her arms and started pacing around the shop.

I adjusted my glasses and opened the paper. She had folded it so that page seven was on top. The social page. There was a nice picture of the stone church near St Stephen's Green with a sharply dressed family coming down the steps, the husband shaking hands with the priest as they left the Sunday service. There was a wife and two small children, a boy and a girl. I noted that neither the wife's hat nor the girl's dress had come from my shop. I looked quickly at the rest of the page and didn't see anything that seemed of particular interest to Doris.

'See?' She jabbed her finger on the page, nearly impaling it. 'Do you see what that slimy shit has been up to?'

'Doris, I don't have a clue what you're on about.'

'Jesus, look at the picture! Don't you see who that is? Bloody Damien!'

'Wha'?' I looked again. Bloody hell, it did look like him, now that I knew what I was looking for. I looked at the caption beneath the photo. 'Mr and Mrs Damien Flannery, with their children Margaret and Robert, leaving Sunday Mass . . .'

I couldn't stop staring at it.

'Do ya see?' Doris stabbed at it again. 'Mr and bloody *Mrs* Flannery – and *their* children! Bloody hell, what about *our* children?'

'My God, he must have been married for years.'

'I know!' She stopped her agitated pacing and slumped onto the edge of a nearby shelf. 'All this time when I thought he was on the road he was really with *them*.'

'Christ.' I looked at her. 'So now what? Can we get him arrested?'

Her lip trembled. 'I don't know. Would that help? Then there'd be two families with the daddy in jail.' She shrugged. 'I don't know what to do.'

We both stared at the newspaper for a while. I didn't know what to tell her: the whole thing seemed insane.

In the end, there was nothing for it but for Doris to carry on with her life and raise the twins on her own. Damien never contacted them again – and he never sent her and the boys so much as a sixpence.

6

The day I gave birth to my second child, I woke up very early with the tell-tale pains and thought, I must get down to the shop and make sure everything is in order.

With my first child, the birthing pains had gone on all day, with nothing much to show for them until the last couple of hours. This seemed like a dreadful waste of time to me. There were things that needed to be sorted before I was 'confined' again for a few days.

So, heavy on my feet, but otherwise feeling not too bad, I popped into Michel's. I wanted to get the new display into the window. With First Communion season coming up, I wanted our dresses and veils to make an eye-catching show. The other girls wouldn't be in for an hour or two, so I had the place to myself. I moved mannequins about, arranged bits and pieces, sorted through some boxes, only occasionally having to stop and take some deep breaths while a contraction skewered through my belly. I was not careless. I only climbed up a very short ladder to finish draping the gauzy material across the top of the window. It framed the whole vignette nicely and was well worth the effort.

I was sorting through some boxes behind the counter when I felt a fiery stab that I thought was going to tear me in two. This was different. Having been through the whole ordeal before, I'd thought I knew what to expect, but this was not at all like what I remembered. This had to be a sign that things were moving along – and fast. Thank goodness the window was tip-top.

I picked up the phone and rang Doris. 'Yeah, so I'll be heading to the hospital soon.'

'Ya will?' She somehow managed to sound bleary-eyed. I don't know how that's done over the phone, but she did it.

'Yes, the baby's coming.'

'Ah, the baby! Christ!' I now heard a flurry of activity at her end that seemed to banish all bleariness.

'So the window here is done and the cash and receipts are all in order. You have someone to help with the driving, yeah?'

'I do. Are you fixed to get to the hospital? Shall I collect you?'

'Not at all.' I reached down and picked up my handbag. Completely unexpectedly a pain shot through me and I made a rather undignified sound into the phone.

'You okay?'

'Yeah, yeah.' I had to lean on the counter a moment. 'Anyway, I'll do just like I did last time. I'll drive myself to the hospital.'

Doris chuckled a bit. 'Fair enough. Does Hughie know you're heading in?'

'I'll phone him when I get there. *Ooooof.*' Damn. Another undignified noise.

'Rio, you don't sound well. I'll come over and take you in.'

'No, no.' I buttoned my cardigan as best as I could and grabbed my handbag again. 'I'm leaving now and I'll be grand. Come and see me in the ward this evening – it'll all be done by then.'

Before she could argue, I hung up and headed out of the door, locking it behind me. As I stepped towards my car, my knees started to buckle.

The first time I'd had a baby, I'd packed myself up at the first twinge and gone to the hospital. It had annoyed the hell out of me that it was ages before anything happened. So this time I had decided to wait till I was much further along before I went anywhere near a hospital. But now everything seemed to be racing forwards.

It occurred to me that I should probably not be behind the wheel if I was going to double over and make 'ooof' noises every five minutes. I straightened up and made for the kerb. Traffic was picking up and before too long I managed to wave down a taxi. As I waddled towards it to open the back door, the driver's eyes widened. I flopped awkwardly into the back seat and pulled the door closed behind me. 'Mount Carmel Hospital, please. *Oooof.*' Damn it, there it was again.

'Right away. Looks like you're ready to go there, missus.'

I was becoming increasingly disinclined to make small-talk.

'Yes. We should – *oooof* – hurry.'

And then I followed with another 'ooof'.

'You got it, missus.'

We tootled along for a few minutes and I felt a bit better. I sat up straighter and looked out of the window. 'Ah, now, you should probably go left up here. You don't want to get stuck in the traffic.'

I saw his eyes flicker to me in the rear-view mirror.

'Yeah, well, we're real close now. It'll just be a few minutes.'

I settled back and closed my eyes, thinking that the next time I opened them we would be at the hospital. Coping with the contractions was taking a lot of my concentration.

I felt the car slowing and thought, Well, we made good time after all. It came to a stop and I opened my eyes. The taxi driver was opening his door and getting out, the engine still running.

How chivalrous! He was going to open the door for me. I felt a surge of warm feeling for the dear man, followed by a contraction. And an 'ooof'.

His door slammed and I was surprised to see him walking away from the car rather than grabbing my door handle. I looked around and was horrified to find that we were parked in front of a small shop. I grabbed the handle, opened the door myself and screamed at his disappearing back, 'What the hell are you doing?'

He turned towards me, while still walking in the direction of the shop. 'Just popping in to get a packet of fags. Won't be a tick.'

'*Are you bloody mad?* I need to go *now*!'

He didn't even look back, just yelled over his shoulder, 'Don't you worry – won't be a minute.'

And off he went into the shop. I couldn't believe it. Jesus, we were still ten minutes from the hospital and the pains were now just a couple of minutes apart.

Another moment. Another spasm. The engine was

running and there was still no sign of the driver. I scooted myself out of the back seat, opened his door and got behind the wheel. With a quick glance in the rear-view mirror, I put the thing into gear.

I can be an impatient driver at the best of times. This was definitely not the best of times. I wove in and out of traffic, I cursed the car (I think his timing belt needed some adjustments), I cursed other drivers, I cursed the traffic, I cursed the weather (it had started to rain and I couldn't figure out how to work the bloody windscreen wipers) and, most of all, I cursed the contractions, which had started to make my eyes water.

With my knees feeling like meaty sacks of jelly, I pulled into the car park at the hospital and stopped the car in a very illegal manner near the entrance. I pulled on the hand-brake and yanked the keys out of the ignition. I opened the door and stood up, then immediately doubled over.

I took a few deep breaths and managed to get myself to the reception desk. The lady there took one look at me, whipped around and yelled for an orderly to bring a wheelchair. I sank into it gratefully. As the young man started to wheel me to the maternity ward I waved at him to stop and then beckoned to the lady at Reception. She ran over to me. 'Yes, love – what can I do for you?'

I handed her the taxi man's car keys. 'Someone is going to come asking for these.'

She looked down into her hand and then at me. I waved at the fella pushing the chair to continue.

Forty-five minutes later, I gave birth to a healthy, cheeky, chubby little boy. We named him Patrick.

The next day, I had an interesting conversation with some police who came to visit me in the hospital, looking for a missing taxi . . .

So now I had two children, and so did Doris. Her husband had abandoned her and as luck – or the lack of it – would have it, my own husband, Hughie, lost his job at the butcher's.

Now cash was a critical problem for both of us. I didn't have enough work for her at my dress shop to be of much help. As careful as she tried to be with her money, and even with some help from her family, I knew Doris was having a hard time of it. There we were, two married women with children, and it was getting difficult to keep all the mouths fed. Our first strategy was to become just about the keenest, shrewdest shoppers you ever saw. We became regulars at the street markets. The bargains were a necessity now, not a lark.

One Saturday, as usual, we were at the Dandelion Market, one of our favourites. I was surprised to see someone from my old neighbourhood there – not shopping, but standing near the back of a van, selling some canned goods out of a stack of boxes. It was Nan, my childhood friend and Tess's older sister.

I trotted over to chat with her, dragging Doris along. I knew Nan had been married a good while back and had a son with health problems. While Doris poked around, I chatted with Nan. I was expecting to see her husband around somewhere, but no – like Doris, Nan had been left on her own, with a handicapped son to raise.

When I asked her how she was getting on, she explained to me that she and Tess would drive the van around, collecting bits and bobs from manufacturers and shops that were getting rid of damaged or cast-off goods. They would get them for a song, then sell them for a very decent profit at the Dandelion and other markets in and around Dublin.

The word 'profit' caught Doris's ear. 'What kinda profits are we talking about?'

Nan looked about, then leaned over and whispered to us how much money she was clearing for herself every week.

'Bloody hell!' Doris stared at her, pop-eyed.

'Well done.' I gave Nan a pat on the arm. 'That's a living wage, all right.'

Nan was all smiles, but was soon busy with other customers so Doris and I moved on.

'Jesus, Rio, there's a fierce amount of money to be made in this street tradin'. Who'da thought?'

'Sure enough. It'd be a lot of work, driving around collecting all the stuff from the wholesalers, mind you.'

Doris stopped and grabbed my elbow. 'Yeah, and here I am with time on my hands.'

'Yeah, so?'

'*You* have a van.'

It was true. I had the old banger of a van for the dress shop.

I grinned. 'Bloody hell! I think we're about to go into the street-tradin' business!'

*

I kept on with my dress shop, but with Doris able to do a lot of the driving, we also got very busy with our market business. The Dandelion was always our favourite, but there were markets up in Finglas, on the north side of the city, as well as in Cork, Limerick, Galway – and all places in between – so we had somewhere to sell things pretty much every day of the week. It would have been unworkable for just one, but with the two of us, there was always someone to mind all of the kids, while the other either drove or did the selling. I had always enjoyed the selling I did at my shop, but the wheeling and dealing we did at the markets was a million times more fun. And it was no secret that neither Doris nor I was much good at being a homebody.

For a good while, we were pretty happy with what we were doing. But we also couldn't help noticing that there were some fellas driving lorries who were selling things in bulk to us street traders, and our hunch was that the bulk selling was where the real money was to be made. Before too long we got the itch to do it ourselves: become lorry-driving wholesalers. It turned out that, from a money-making perspective, we were spot on. That was definitely where the biggest profits were, with the quickest turnaround. There was only one problem: women couldn't be lorry drivers.

That was what we were told. The Republic of Ireland would not let a woman take the Heavy Goods Vehicle (HGV) licence training, let alone the actual test. When I informed Doris about this obstacle to our ambitions, she came up with an elaborate plan that would have permanently affected the reproductive abilities of every man in the entire motor-vehicle department (and resulted in some other interesting anatomical changes), but unfortunately, it wouldn't actually get us licensed.

My own opinion was that I had never heard such a load of rubbish in all my life. I got on the phone and talked to everyone I could think of who knew anything about driving lorries or getting a licence, and I came up with a brilliant idea: we would get licensed in Northern Ireland. It turned out there were already some women with HGV licences in the North. The barrier had already been broken there.

Doris and I had a couple of months of lessons with some local lorry men, then took our tests in Northern Ireland. Next thing we knew, we were the first women in our part of the country to be licensed lorry drivers.

Now that we could get on the road and do some serious hauling, the money increased quite a lot. But, then, so did the amount of time we had to put into the business. I gave up Michel's and dedicated myself to trading full-time. Doris and I worked out a routine: when one of us was on the road with the lorry, the other stayed at home and minded all of the kids. Sometimes we even took one or two of the kids with us, especially as they got older.

So there we were. Two lorry-drivin' mamas. We were no longer scrounging from market to market on Saturdays and Sundays in our van. Now we had all of Ireland – and beyond – for trading, selling, bargaining and bartering. It was heaven.

PART TWO

From Mother to Field Marshal

The one piece of advice I always give is: become a foster parent because you want to help the child. Not because you expect the child to think of you as their mother or father. Or to love you for the rest of their lives. They might never love you. But you have to do the very best you can for them at all times, no matter what. Fostering is one of the few jobs where your ultimate goal is not to be needed any more.

7

The asphalt trembled under the lorry wheels, and the gear lever shuddered comfortably in my left hand. The sky was a streaky blue, driving conditions were good, and just a few miles ahead was one of my favourite cafés. I loved these hours. The busy part of the work was over. Now it was just hauling the twenty-foot trailer home. A stop for a bite to eat, some strong coffee, and a chat with Adèle. Then a straight shot to Le Havre, on to the ferry and home.

I slowed at a small junction and changed down as I drove around a bend in the road to the right. A middle-aged Frenchman, his small dog at the end of a lead, a newspaper under his arm, had looked up as the whining engine breezed past him. When he saw my curly head smiling at him from the cab window, the poor man nearly dropped everything – his jaw especially.

I nodded at him, still grinning toothily. The man's horror at seeing a woman behind the wheel was delicious. But the time I had to savour my small triumph was short – there was the café, and under the striped awning I could see Adèle. She was clearing some dishes and talking to someone, though I couldn't see who.

After parking the lorry next to the village petrol station, I crossed the road and saw a bushy stand of untidy brown hair bristling above a table top as Adèle leaned over to give its owner a spoon. A tiny hand shot out and I knew who it was. I walked into the shade of the awning and headed for her.

'So the scamps are back, are they?'

Adèle turned. 'Of course. And they are very hungry.'

As I pulled out a chair and sat down, I peered over the table edge. Sitting cross-legged on the ground, bowls in their laps, spoons in their hands, were two of the filthiest children I had ever seen. 'Christ.' I hadn't meant to say it in front of the boys, but, well . . . they looked awful.

Adèle wiped her hands on her apron and shoved a basket of bread towards the sound of the soup being slurped. 'I know,' she said. 'It is very bad this time. They came not for the begging of money but for food. They don't know where their *maman* is.'

I picked up two rolls from the basket and handed them to the boys. They were snatched so quickly it was like being snapped at by sharks. I leaned down to the older of the two – I couldn't pronounce his name so I just called him Jackie.

'So how're ya gettin' on?'

He looked back at me blankly and kept chewing. His face was shiny with dirt, his clothes soiled, rumpled and emitting a ferocious smell.

His younger brother gazed at me briefly and I was shocked to see that his eyes were gooey and crusted. He blinked very hard and coughed; it was a thin cough that sounded like pebbles dropped into a dusty jar. It was as if he didn't have the strength even to cough properly. Something about the fevered, feeble timidity of it scared me.

Adèle seemed to have felt it, too. 'The little one, he is sick. I think it might be bad.'

I grabbed two more rolls and handed them to Jackie. Without a pause, he stuck one in his mouth and handed the other immediately to his brother. I smiled. That was why I had always liked them. They were obnoxious little buggers sometimes, hanging about the café, begging for small change. They weren't above reaching into a handbag or a pocket either. But it was only change they were after: they were not dedicated thieves.

Their mother, lolling at home in her alcoholic stew, had ordered them to go out and bring back change and that was what they did.

At seven years old, and with a brother to care for, Jackie was unable to do anything beyond what he had been told to do. He brought home the change, and he kept his brother as fed and safe as he could. Over the past few months, I had known it was a bad situation. But now something had changed.

'How long have they been like this?'

Adèle wiped her hands on her apron. 'I am not sure. Perhaps a week? I did not know until two days ago that they had nowhere to sleep. Last night I let them sleep in the shed.'

I didn't speak much French but decided to try a little. I leaned down to Jackie. '*Où est la maman?*'

Jackie looked at me thoughtfully, digesting both his

bread and the awful French. He shrugged, waved one hand in a dismissive gesture and went back to his soup.

Adèle decided this would take some time so she sat down next to me. The only other customers were a couple sitting at a table on the other side of the patio, half-empty coffee cups in front of them, engrossed in a conversation that, from what I had overheard, had something to do with *l'amour* and *l'argent*. Always a bad combination.

'They tell me she is not at home and that home is closed. They cannot get in.'

'They're locked out?'

Adèle considered for a moment. 'I believe it is more. Everything is gone.'

'Did their mother take everything and move?'

'Perhaps. I think it was all taken by the landlord. I don't know what you say in English.'

I contemplated Jackie's dirty, bushy head. 'Sounds like they were evicted.'

'Ah, as you say.'

'And I would also say it seems their mother is a right bitch and has scarpered without telling them where she was going.'

Adèle shrugged.

'What about other relatives? Grandma? Aunts? A big fat rich uncle?'

'I asked.' Adèle gathered up the bread basket. 'They don't know of anyone.'

I took the bread basket back and handed it to Jackie. 'How long can they stay with you?'

Adèle stopped halfway to reaching for the basket again.

'They can stay a long time – but it is not good for them to sleep in the shed, no?'

I stared at her. I am sure that she felt the uncomfortable self-consciousness one would feel if caught under a microscope, swimming about on a glass slide. 'Is that the best you can do? Let them sleep in your shed?'

'I am sorry.' Adèle snatched the bread basket back decisively. 'Yes, it is the best I can do.'

Settling for winning the skirmish rather than the entire war, she retreated to the kitchen.

I looked down thoughtfully at the boys' heads as they were mopping the bottoms of their soup bowls with the last pieces of bread. '*Alors*, boys. How about if you come and stay with your auntie Rio for a bit?'

Jackie peered up at me. He seemed to be thinking that I had done a real good job getting them the extra bread. He had to admire that – it was the kind of sleight of hand he and his brother depended on for themselves. He gave me a cheeky grin.

Well, I thought, I'll take that for a yes.

Once we were on the road and the excitement (or the sugar – I had bought the boys some sweets for the trip) had worn off, the boys were delighted to crawl into the bed built into the cabin of the truck. It was above and behind my head on a shelf, hidden behind a hinged drop-down door.

An hour and a half later, the lorry was in the queue at the ferry landing in Le Havre.

As I drove up to hand over my ticket and papers, I noticed the man's eyes flicker across the front seat. The hinged door over the bed stayed closed and the boys were completely silent. As my papers were put back into my hand and I was waved on through, I finally exhaled.

I didn't know if anyone on the ferry would care that I had two pint-sized extra passengers but I didn't want to find out.

Once I'd got the rig squared away, I knocked on the hinged door and swung it open. Jackie looked at me expectantly. His younger brother (what was I going to call him? Adèle had told me his name but it was unpronounceable) seemed a bit drowsy. And he still had some crust on his eyelashes.

'Come on, you two! Let's stretch our legs!'

Amazing how a tone of voice and the right hand-gestures can compensate for language. The boys jumped down and followed me up the stairs to the passenger decks.

When they passed a large picture window, the boys stopped as if they'd been smacked. They stood for a moment in dead silence, then the younger one grabbed Jackie's arm and started babbling excitedly. Jackie was shaking his head and babbling back.

He turned to me, just as his brother was starting to sound hysterical. His eyes were huge.

He said something – it sounded, based on my limited French, as if he was asking, 'Where?' As in, perhaps, 'Where are we?'

Tears were now dribbling down his brother's face, mingling with the crust and the ever-present snot.

The boys were staring at the expanse of dark, dingy, seemingly endless water with something between terror and disbelief.

Well, I thought. This could be interesting.

I don't know why, but I'd just assumed it would be easy to sort the boys out (Doris would say this was typical of me, to go in head first and do the thinking later). But it was nearly two years before I could send them home to join their family.

Our local parish priest, Father Neary, was a real life-saver. Not only did he speak pretty passable French but he helped me organize things with the Salvation Army so that we could track down their aunt and grandmother. Poor things, the women had been frantic trying to find the lads. The grandmother had discovered somehow that the mother had scarpered and had sent for the boys to come and stay with her. And then things had got a bit strange.

Unable to speak French, I had relied on Adèle to do the translating for me and had already seen that she tended to edit what she said. And by 'edit', I mean that she would leave out big chunks of information that might be important. For example, she had told the boys that they were going to go home with me for a while but had failed to mention that my home was in Ireland. I would have thought that was rather important.

Then I found out that when the police had come to the village to collect the boys for their frantic grandmother, who was searching for them, poor Adèle had panicked. I had given her all of my contact information just in case someone came looking for them. The sight of the uni-forms, however, apparently made her wonder if perhaps she shouldn't have let the lads go off with someone she hardly knew who lived in another country. Not sure where she would stand in the whole thing, she had played it safe and told the police nothing. She acted like she didn't know anything at all and they went away.

I suppose I can't blame her for that. But, unfortunately, she also didn't think to contact me and let me know that someone had come looking for them. Although the story had a happy ending, it would have been happy sooner if we hadn't had to spend so much time trying to track their family down. But, all in all, the two of them had a great time while they lived with me. They went to school, they learned English — with pure Dublin accents, the way it should be spoken! — and made loads of friends.

I had tried to do everything right — I had reported that the boys were staying with me to Father Neary and to the local police. I made it clear that they were just staying with me until we could find some responsible family members who would care for them properly. When we finally took them back across the water, to relatives in Portugal, it was a bittersweet journey, early in the summer. But after I'd met their granny and their aunt, the mother's sister who lived with her, I knew that the children would have the care they needed. It seemed to me, as I headed back to Ireland, that all was right with the world.

8

With the amount of time that Doris and I spent on the road, it seemed only logical to make the lorry as comfortable as possible. We had the little bunk in the front cabin, which was fine when you needed to pull over for a quick nap. And rather than stay at inns or hotels when we had a long haul, we fitted out the back end of the lorry with a mat and a sleeping-bag, a gas ring that we fuelled from a propane tank and a cooler full of basic foodstuffs. There was even a small table. It was, in many ways, a true home from home.

Word got out about the two women (and occasionally their kids) who were traipsing about the countryside in a kitted-out lorry. At first the other drivers kind of avoided us, or treated us like we had something contagious. But after a while curiosity got the better of them and we found ourselves sharing a mug of tea out of the back with fellow traders and truckers. One fella in the Finglas market in particular, a bear of a man named Robbie, became a particularly good friend. He was the first to make us feel welcome there and also the first to realize that our truck might be a haven for some of the destitute folks he was forever rescuing – or chasing off, sometimes both – from the market stalls of a morning.

The first time he came to me, he had with him a teen-aged lad who had started out by pilfering the occasional apple or some cheese, then had started stealing kettles, radios and other stuff that he could sell. Robbie had every intention of dragging him off by one ear, until he discovered that the boy was homeless and slept in a nearby alley. Big and bear-like he might have been, but Robbie was a fair-minded man. He brought the lad to me whenever I was at the market and I would let him sleep in the back, where he would be dry and safe, then give him tea and a bacon sandwich when he woke up. Eventually the lad found a job (with Robbie's help) working for one of the traders he used to steal from. It might seem crazy, these days, but back then it made perfect sense. The boy wasn't a criminal, he had just had a load of bad luck, and once he'd found his feet, he turned into a dependable, hardworking young man who never forgot the folks who'd helped him.

It was no skin off my nose to help that fella, and I'd been glad to do it. So I wasn't too surprised when Robbie showed up one morning with a couple of young boys. He asked if they could kip in the back of the truck as they'd been sleeping rough. Well, it was one thing to hear about a seventeen-year-old lad living like that – but these two boys, who were brothers, were just aged ten and twelve. And they looked like they had been sleeping rough for a good while. I couldn't believe it.

I got the boys – Jimmy and Ted – fed and settled. It was hard to tell if they were too sleepy to eat or too hungry to sleep – both seemed a struggle. But once I'd got some milk and sandwiches into them, and they seemed to understand that the back of the truck was a perfectly safe place to be, they snuggled into the sleeping-bags and were off to Dreamland.

I went back out front and cornered Robbie. 'Jaysus, what's the story here, Rob? Why are ones so young living like this around here?'

He scratched his stubbly chin and wagged his head. 'I know, I know. It's a sad state of affairs, it is. I'd seen them for a few days, sleeping under some of the stalls. Took me a good while to get close enough to nab them. I haven't been able to figure out much, just that they got turfed out of where they'd been living.'

'Well, I'm out of here at six this evening. That can't be helped.'

'I know, I know.' His head was still wagging. 'Just let them stay in there till then, can you? They really don't get much rest on the street – they can't ever get completely comfortable, ya know?'

'I think you're misunderstanding me.' I was a foot shorter than Robbie, but I did my best to glare up at him over my glasses. 'I'm not turning those boys loose on the street when it gets dark this evening. When they wake up, you need to explain to them that I'm taking them back to my place tonight.'

He squinted down at me. 'Can you do that? Just take them off with you?'

'Well, if their own parents can turn them out to forage in the gutter, I should hope it isn't some sort of crime to give poor starving boys a hot meal and a roof over their heads! You'd better believe I can bloody well do it.'

I didn't bother to mention that I'd done it before.

I kept glaring, waiting to see what he would do. He grinned back at me, slapped a paw on my shoulder and said, 'Fair play. I'm delighted you'll help.'

I was delighted, too. I was getting a major pain in my neck glaring up at him and his big hairy chin. I jabbed a finger into his ample gut. 'Meanwhile, you need to do some digging.'

That made him one unhappy bear. 'What kind of digging?'

'You need to find out where they came from. They must be from around here somewhere.'

That seemed to be the kind of digging Robbie was willing to do.

'All right so, will do.' He gave me a mock salute and ambled off.

Later on, he had a chat with the boys. They seemed a bit alarmed at the prospect of heading out with me, but I promised them it was just temporary, that they would be back in Finglas in no time. This promise, and a promise of a hot meal, seemed to do the trick. Once we got home, I also suggested baths all round. It's a sign of how desperate a state they were in that those two boys were delighted at the prospect of a bath!

The next morning I rang Social Services and told them where I had found the boys, the condition they were in, and that they were staying with me. I had half expected someone there to know who they were, for there already to be a case file on them.

But no. Sadly, it is completely possible for two children who shouldn't be expected to fend for themselves to be kicked out into the streets and no one any the wiser. That's how some of those people who call themselves parents get away with it, I suppose.

I knew that, eventually, the Social Services people would track down Jimmy and Ted's family. Especially after Robbie had found some locals who knew something about the boys and their situation. But 'eventually' wasn't good enough for me. I didn't want to hound the poor lads, but I wanted to know what was going on.

At tea the next evening, after I had filled them up with shepherd's pie and Jaffa cakes, I started a process that I call 'asking questions'. Doris informed me later that this process was more aptly referred to as 'sticking my nose in where it doesn't belong'. Call it what you will, it gets results.

I've seen it many times since, but this was early days for me and the first time I witnessed how protective children can be of the very people who are making them miserable. Call someone 'mother' or 'father' and, to their own children, it provides a sort of cloak of perfection. They can do no wrong, no matter how much wrong they're doing.

Jimmy, the older one, told me why they were living the way they were. Their dad had left about five years earlier and since that time their mum's 'bouts', as he called them, had become more frequent.

I had to have him explain that to me.

Apparently their ma could plod along just fine for a while, might even get a part-time job somewhere – in a shop or a market stall or cleaning pubs. But then her 'bout' would start: she would buy massive amounts of alcohol and invite everyone she knew to her place and start a booze-up that would go on for days. I found out later that these weren't really friends she was inviting in: she was bringing in people off the streets, people she had just met, people who were not the sort that should be in a home with young children. And I also found out that these parties weren't just boozers: there were drugs and all kinds of behaviour that . . . Well, let's just say it was a good thing that their mum had had enough sense to realize the boys should not be around. In her own befuddled way, she protected them from the worst of it.

So, over the past few years, Jimmy and Ted had become accustomed to the cycle of relative normality and then – boom! They had to be out of the way and take care of themselves until Mum's binge was over. Sometimes it was a few days. At other times it was a few weeks.

In our new enlightened age, we would probably say that their mum was bipolar, but back then, there wasn't a polite term for it. All I knew was that she and the lads needed help.

What struck me most as I sat at my kitchen table listening to Jimmy explain this to me was how matter-of-fact he was about the whole thing. How accepting. As if this was normal. They had both missed a lot of school and I suppose they didn't have enough interaction with kids from 'ordinary' families to understand that this was not how things were supposed to be. They were grateful for my help. But in some odd way Jimmy, as the elder boy, seemed to think that his failure to provide well for him and his brother during their mum's bouts was his fault. As if, at the age of twelve, he should have been able to do better.

His unquestioning loyalty to his mother broke my heart. I knew that it was very unlikely that Social Services would ever let the boys go home while their mum was in such an unpredictable state. I knew it was the best thing in the world to keep them away from her. And I also knew that being separated from her would shatter them almost as much as the abuse had done.

Sure enough, within a couple of weeks, the Social Services folks got back to me and said that they had located the boys' aunt in Limerick and she was delighted to take them in.

Jimmy stared at me when I told him this news with eyes that would have frozen a teardrop. Ted was certainly shedding quite a few. 'You promised us,' Jimmy said to me.

I didn't know what he meant. What had I promised other than a bed, a meal and some help?

'Sorry, love, but what did I promise?'

'You promised we would go back to Finglas.'

Ah. I had, hadn't I?

'I'm so sorry, love, but there's no one to take care of you there. I thought I'd be able to take you back, but I can't.'

'Our ma is there. Of course someone's there.' He was angry and Ted was whimpering. God, how had this gone so horribly wrong?

'Your ma is not well enough to care for you, you know that.' I patted his shoulder. 'She loves you, of course she does. She just isn't able to be a good mam for you right now. Maybe soon she will.'

He looked up at me very sharply. 'D'ya think so – soon?'

God help me, there I was telling a lie to this poor boy who already had been through hell.

'Sure and why not? Just be patient and give your ma a chance to get really better.'

Which seemed about as likely as monkeys playing banjos, but I couldn't tell him that. If the little lie gave him hope and eased his mind a bit, then so be it. They got into the car with the social worker and went off to Limerick.

Their mother, despite treatment, rehab, detox and God knew what all else, never got better and disappeared after about eighteen months. No one knows where she got to or if she's still alive.

I never heard from Jimmy or Ted. The social worker told me, about six months later, that they had settled in well with their aunt – but still constantly asked about going back to their mother. I wrote a couple of letters to them, asking them how they were getting on, but got no answer. I suppose they never forgave me for not taking them back to Finglas.

It was my first taste of how much it can hurt when all you want to do is help. As Doris pointed out, if you're going to stick your nose in, sometimes you'll find you've stuck it into a wasps' nest.

Meanwhile, Robbie brought his down-and-outers to us, off and on, for all the years that we were trading at the Finglas market. And I never learned to keep my nose out, wasps or no.

9

My lorry, parked in the Finglas market on a Sunday morning, should have been named Shelter Central, but that was all right with me. People who needed a spell out of the weather and a mug of tea to take the sting off, well, I had no problem with that.

Then there was the morning that Robbie brought me Susan.

She didn't look any different from the other hardscrabblers he'd brought my way. She carried a large bag on her shoulder that I guessed contained pretty much everything she owned. She wasn't particularly grubby – in fact, she was wearing makeup – but her hair was greasy and her clothes looked slept in. She might just have been a party-loving girl who had been out on a good old long night out.

Except that she was only fourteen.

The makeup and packet of cigarettes in her pocket didn't fool me.

I admit, I was a bit off-hand with her at first. She seemed, in many ways, just like every other kid Robbie had brought to me. Living rough for some reason that I would ferret out. And then, after ferreting it out, I'd get her sorted and we'd all live happily ever after. That was always the plan.

But, ah, the best-laid plans . . .

At any rate, it all started out as the usual. Robbie brought her to me with the usual story that she just needed a place to sleep and a bite to eat. So she got the usual mug of tea, bacon sandwich and the use of the sleeping-bag.

After she'd had a rest, and the lads and I had packed up the lorry after the market closed, I made her another mug of tea and we had a chat. 'So, where will ya be off to now? You got somewhere for tonight?'

She tucked her lank hair behind her ears, put a cigarette into her mouth and leaned forward to light it on the gas ring. She inhaled and shrugged.

'If ya don't mind my asking,' I knew there was a fat chance of that, 'why are you out on your own? Where's Mammy and Daddy?'

She eyed me as if she was trying to figure me. It was a shock to see it in such a young girl, but it was the same kind of sharp-eyed appraisal I was used to seeing when I dealt with grizzled old traders. That kind of weighing-up to determine if I was going to be an easy mark and, if so, how much I could be swindled for, or if I'd be a tough nut to crack. I did the same thing myself. Takes one to know one, as they say. I couldn't help but wonder which way she had weighed me – simple sap or not someone to mess with?

'I got no ma,' she finally answered, tapping her cigarette ash into her empty mug.

I had to bite my lip because I wanted to smack her hand. 'Sorry to hear that, love.'

She shrugged, like it didn't matter. 'She died a coupla years ago. Cancer.'

I just nodded. Not much you can say to that. 'Sorry' never seems to be enough. 'Brothers or sisters?'

She shook her head.

'And your da? Surely he's looking for ya, wondering where ya are.'

Again, just a shrug. 'He knows where I am.'

I wasn't having that. 'What do you mean he knows where ya are? He knows you're out scrounging meals in the back of a lorry parked at the Sunday market?'

That made her grin. 'Nah, he knows not to worry. He lives not too far from here. He knows I never leave the neighbourhood.'

I'm surprised my glasses didn't steam over. The idea that her father would know that she was living on the streets yet do nothing about it made me furious – and disgusted. My own daughter, Gwen, was of a similar age by then. The idea that she would be running around, day and night, and I didn't know exactly where she was or what she was doing was incomprehensible to me. How could her own father not care? How could he be so unconcerned with the obvious dangers to a girl of her age? I wanted to go to his home at that very moment and shove my foot very far up a place where boots normally never went, my hope being that he would end up with his you-know-whats where his tonsils should be.

We chatted a bit more. She wasn't going to school regularly (one more reason for me to put my boot into her father's bits): school was 'boring', and none of her friends were there, and she hated the teachers, and never learned anything useful – she had a good long list of the usual excuses. So she would skip out and stay a night or two with various friends (the ones she preferred to her school mates, apparently) and 'acquaintances' (I found that to be particularly chilling), but she had nowhere to go that night. She couldn't – or wouldn't – go home. I reined in my imagination as I didn't want to contemplate all of the reasons why she might feel she couldn't spend the night in her own home.

So I did my usual, and told her she could come and stay with me. Rather than look delighted (which I had hoped for), or at least relieved, she was alarmed. 'But I'll need to get back here tomorrow.'

'Why?' I wasn't afraid to ask and she seemed taken aback.

'Well . . . I . . . em . . . I have things here I need to take care of.'

Good Lord, was she referring to her father? Was she, in some random way, taking care of the miserable bastard? That nearly sent me round the bend.

'Susan, if we need to get you back here, we will, don't you worry.'

She still seemed hesitant.

'Susan, look at the state you're in. If you can't go home, you at least need to spend the night somewhere safe.'

It had started to rain, so the prospect of a proper roof over her head won out over her other worries and she agreed to come with me.

And so the adventure began.

Back at my place, I got Susan sorted in a room that she shared with Gwen and Rose. My kids were so used to me bringing people home that they didn't bat an eyelid. People often ask me what my own family thought of all of my carryings-on, and the answer is that they never knew any other way to live. It had been going on since before they were born and it was just what we did all the time. Everyone was prepared to set up an extra cot, get out another clean towel, shove down and make room at the dinner table. Years later, when they were grown and out in the world, I suspect it was a shock to my children that everyone else didn't constantly bring strangers home and raise them as if they were one of their own. But it seemed normal to us.

The next day I explained to Susan that she was welcome to wash whatever clothes she had in her bag and help herself to whatever was in the kitchen while I went to 'work'. Actually, Doris had the lorry that day and was off to Wexford. Instead I drove the van over to Finglas and followed the leads Robbie had given me about Susan's dad.

I had my boots on and I was ready to shove them somewhere.

According to the information Robbie had dug up, I would find Noel, Susan's father, at home in the afternoon as he was on evening shift work. Well, at least he had a job.

I went to the neighbourhood where he was supposed to be, asked around and was directed to what turned out to be a neat, orderly row of houses. I had been expecting something much more rancid. But appearances can be deceiving. I knocked on the door and braced myself for a fight.

When the door opened I blinked at the tall, thin, bespectacled man, who blinked right back at me.

'Are you Noel McCarty?' I must have sounded like I was going to arrest him.

He was dressed in clean, presentable clothes and did not reek of alcohol. Nor did he have beady eyes or look shifty. I was finding this perplexing.

'Yes, I am. Can I help you?'

Damn it. Polite, too. It was going to be difficult to get my boot into this one.

'My name is Rio Hogarty and I have your daughter Susan staying with me in Clondalkin.'

'Oh, I see! Please come in.'

He didn't seem overjoyed to see me. Or particularly surprised. He had an air of resignation, as if this had happened before. He didn't seem to like it, but had become used to it.

I went inside and found a homely living room that was standing to full attention. Tidy and spotless. But then, I reminded myself, abusive, neglectful people can also be tidy. I was determined not to let the good impression his home had made sway me from my purpose.

He sat down and I sat across from him. I scanned the room and noticed the photos of his wife and a small girl – Susan, no doubt – scattered about.

'Susan told me she was staying with someone, but I didn't know who it was.' He ran his hand through his thin, grey hair and I noticed his fingers were trembling a bit.

'She told you?' This was news to me.

'Yes, she rang me this morning. She never tells me much, but at least I know she's okay.'

I wondered when the little minx had made her call from my kitchen phone – I hadn't seen her do it. 'Mr McCarty, does it not bother you that your fourteen-year-old daughter is running around the town sleeping here and there and doing God knows what?' My voice started to rise and I fought to keep my feet out of kicking range.

He smiled, but it was not because he was happy.

'Of course, Mrs Hogarty. Of course it does. But I've tried everything. She refuses to stay here, no matter what I do.'

This bothered me. There are many reasons I can think of as to why a young girl who is an only child may not want to stay alone with her father. I realized I might have to be sick before I could start any actual violence. The look I gave him must have spoken volumes.

'Since Susan's mother died, I've done everything I could to provide a good home for her.' He stared for a moment at his clasped hands. 'But she started running about with some kids who steered her in a different direction. I've tried everything, but I can't watch her twenty-four hours a day.'

'Well, letting her run wild isn't the answer. Surely you can see that. She's not even going to school.'

He winced. I couldn't have done better if I'd slapped him. But somehow it wasn't very satisfying.

'I know. I've been over all this with the school, and the social worker, and the minder I hired to stay with her.'

This was news. So far, it sounded like he'd been trying to do everything right. What was going on here?

'I'm as ashamed as I can be, Mrs Hogarty.'

'Call me Rio.' I hadn't meant to say that.

'Well, Rio – I'm ashamed to say that I've been unable to control my own daughter. And no one else has been able to help me. The only thing I've been able to work out with her is that when she isn't home she calls me once a day and lets me know she's all right.'

'So sometimes she is home?'

'Oh, yes. She'll be home for days at a time – and then one day she'll just take off. I can never figure out what makes her go.'

He seemed too tired and sad even to cry.

'Well, she's at my place for now. Perhaps the change of scenery will do her good. And I have a couple of girls close to her age. Maybe that will help. If you'd like, I'll see if I can get her to go to school with them.'

'Yes, yes – please do.' He looked me in the eye. 'You must think I'm a terrible father.'

'Not at all, Mr McCarty. It sounds like you're doing your best.'

Mind you, what I was really thinking was that I was going to call Susan's school in Finglas and Social Services and see if his story checked out. Because if it didn't, my boots and I would be back.

So off I went, sticking my nose into all sorts of places. Sure enough, everyone I talked to – the teachers at Susan's school, the social worker, even the local parish priest – all had nothing but good things to say about Noel. Reviews of Susan were less positive.

Apparently, within a year after her mother had died she'd started hanging around with some older kids in her

84

neighbourhood who were described as 'the wrong sort'. Truancy from school and general misbehaviour resulted. It had been an ongoing struggle for her father ever since.

I was convinced that I could help. It seemed to me that living in a busy household with girls close to her own age would be just what Susan needed so that she could get involved with a new crowd of more appropriate companions. I had found her in the nick of time. I would save her – and save her relationship with her heartbroken father. Rio to the rescue.

Over the next few weeks, Susan seemed to accept that she would be staying with us for a while. She even put on her uniform and went to school for several days. I thought she went to school for several weeks, but one day I got a phone call from the headmaster and I was informed that Susan had not been seen for more than ten days. Was she ill?

I stammered some excuse, hung up and tried to figure out how she had been managing it. She had been getting up every morning, making her packed lunch, and heading out – in her uniform! – with the other kids. But, of course, none of my children was in her class. What she did after she got there, no one knew.

When she showed up at the house later that afternoon, I gave her an earful. I went through her schoolbag and found cigarettes, nylon stockings, a pair of high heels, some cash, and some bits and pieces of tin foil that I assumed came from chocolates.

She was a clever one. First she protested her innocence and had all sorts of excuses. Then she started screaming and yelling about how I wasn't her mother and I couldn't tell her what to do. When that didn't work, she tried crying. I let her get it all out of her system. When she finally slipped into sullen silence, I explained to her that I was going to ask my girls to check in with someone in her class every day and find out if she was there. If I heard that she wasn't, there would be hell to pay.

She didn't exactly accept this, but she didn't argue with me either. She just stormed upstairs and we didn't see her until dinner. She never missed a meal. I expected a storm cloud at the dinner table, but instead she was deliberately chirpy and cheerful, acting as if nothing had happened. She even helped with the dishes. I thought my handling of the situation had turned out to be brilliant.

Next day she was off to school again – after I had checked that she had nothing in her bag except books and her lunch. She accepted my search with good grace.

At the end of the day, Gwen and Rose were home at their usual time. They informed me that their contact in Susan's class had told them she had disappeared before lunch.

I can't say I was entirely surprised, but it still made me very angry. She was obviously trying to see how far she could push me. Well, we would just find out.

For the rest of the afternoon, every time the front door opened (which was frequently, as is usual at my house), I braced myself for a confrontation. But every time it wasn't her. Supper time came and went. And then it was evening, and still no sign of her. Damn.

I marshalled everyone I could think of – my kids, the neighbours, Doris, and some of the lads who worked with us at the markets – and we combed the neighbourhood. We checked houses, shops, bus stops – even pubs. Not a trace of her. I rang the police and reported what had happened. I rang her father to tell him, but he was at work and in those days we didn't have answering machines. I was hoping that before morning we would find her and I wouldn't have to tell him that I had lost his daughter.

The night dragged on, with friends, relatives and police combing the area. Morning came and the kids headed off to school. Still no sign of Susan. I felt sick to my stomach. I got into my van and went out driving everywhere I could think of – the park, some dismal alleyways, along the canal – then decided to head towards Finglas. Maybe she'd tried to make her way there.

I managed to get to her neighbourhood, scouring the streets and footpaths, and decided I had better tell her father face to face. I knocked on his door and had to steel myself. I dreaded that door opening and seeing him more than anything I had ever dreaded in my life. I wasn't even sure what words I could use to explain to him that the police were trying to find his little girl.

When he opened the door, he smiled. 'Ah, Rio! Didn't expect to see you here.'

I really wished he would stop smiling.

'Listen, it's about Susan . . .' I hesitated, not sure what I could follow that with. She ran away? I lost her? I chased her off? I failed to protect her?

He spoke before I had to say anything. 'Not to worry,' he said. 'It's fine for her to stay here for a bit. She's promised me she'll go back to school. Would you like to come in?'

The door opened wider but I couldn't move. My lower jaw was hanging like a useless plank. 'Is she here?' I finally managed to squeak.

'Of course. She appeared early this morning. Said she was homesick.' He leaned his head back and looked at me very intently through his glasses. 'Did she not tell you?'

I was fuming now. I went from torturous embarrassment to less than noble rage in about five seconds flat. 'No, she did not.' I was too angry even to shout.

He laughed a little. Like it was some cute trick Susan had played. I was rapidly getting back to wanting to stick a boot in him.

'I'm so sorry, I assumed you knew.'

I stood there for a minute, just glaring at him. His easy-going smile visibly faltered. 'Would you like to see her? She was very tired when she got here – she's been sleeping for a while now.'

I shoved him aside with an elbow and marched in. 'Yes, I would like to see her.' I turned to glare at him some more and waited so that he could show me where her room was.

I stomped up the stairs and threw the door open, ready to start a tongue-lashing that might leave her with nothing but her hide. But she was sound asleep, wrapped up in a very girlish pink eiderdown. I just stood there, torn between wanting to tuck her in or give her a very loud account of all the aggravation she had caused. I just stared at her for a moment, then stepped back and closed her door.

Noel looked sheepish. 'I'm so sorry.' He was practically wringing his hands. 'I just thought you knew.'

'Not to worry.' I allowed myself to feel relieved that she was all right. 'As long as she's safe and sound, that's the important thing.' I pushed my glasses up my nose and gave him a partial glare. 'But she gave us one hell of a fright.'

As calmly as I could, I asked him to ring the police and explain what had happened.

Her stay with her dad lasted a couple of weeks. Then she ran off – who knows where? – and showed up at the lorry on a Sunday at the market. She had all kinds of excuses and she made all kinds of promises. She looked thin and unwell and it seemed, once again, that she had nowhere else to go. Or, at least, nowhere else she wanted to go. I suspected that she had burned a few bridges with her father.

What could I do? I took her back. And we tried again. School uniform and all.

But within a week it wasn't the headmaster who rang. One afternoon there was a knock at my front door and there was a policeman – holding Susan by the elbow.

I had to look twice to make sure it was her. She had on more makeup than I'd known she owned, her school skirt was rolled up so short around her waist it barely made a decent belt, and she had on a pair of high-heeled lace-up boots.

He brought her into the house and gave me the bad news. Susan had been caught shoplifting. I was absolutely mortified. She was making circles with her finger on the tablecloth and refused to look at me. The long and the short of it was that it was her first offence and the amount she had taken (some cheap jewellery) was not large, so they were letting her off with a warning. But she was not to go into that shop again or she would be arrested. She actually smirked when he said that.

After the policeman left, I sat down across from her. 'Why'd you do it? If you wanted some bangles, why didn't you just ask me?'

She sniffed. 'I didn't want the bloody stuff. I nicked it so's I could sell it. I wanted some cash.'

'What happened to your pocket money for this week? How could you have spent that already?'

'It's none of your business what I do with my money!' She slammed her hand on the table and stood up. 'You don't understand what I need!' She stormed out of the kitchen and ran up the stairs.

After that, I realized why her father had stopped pressuring her to go to school. If I had gone with her every day and physically tied her to a desk, or sat on her so she couldn't leave, we could probably have made her stay. But short of that, there was no way to persuade her to attend.

I started letting her help with the marketing business. That lasted only a few days – she was not interested in getting up early in the morning, even if she could have a breakfast roll and a kip in the back of the lorry. I didn't want to leave her at home all day, but I didn't want her running around either. A friend of mine hired her to work a couple of hours in the evening cleaning offices. I thought the hours would suit her. It seemed to be just the ticket – she could sleep late and go to work after dinner. She seemed delighted with herself for the first couple of weeks, cheerful and eager to go to work. I should have known that wasn't a good sign.

Sure enough, I eventually got the phone call from my friend – Susan had only shown up for work a couple of times. And I found out that when I thought she had come home from 'work', she was actually just pretending to be home for the night. She would get up again in the wee hours, sneak out of the house and go out with a gang I wouldn't have let Hitler's kids hang out with.

I sat her down and told her I knew what was going on. She dropped the cheerful act right away. She spat some venomous words at me, stormed off – and the next day she was gone.

Again.

I knew I couldn't round everybody up to look for her after what had happened last time. Instead I waited a few hours, then rang her dad. Sure enough, that was where she had landed. She stayed with him for a few days, and when that thrill had worn off, or she'd got bored, she showed up again on my doorstep. Where she had been between the time she left her dad's and got to my place was anyone's guess.

She was scrubbed clean, wearing sensible shoes, and had a contrite expression on her face. She came back in with us, only to have the cycle start all over again.

This went on for a couple of years. She would go to school occasionally. Then, when she stopped going, I had a neighbour come to the house and help her with her schoolwork. That would always start well, then become a disaster. I would find things for her to do; she would half-heartedly try them, give up, start hanging out with undesirables again, then go back to her dad's for a few days, only to reappear on my doorstep some time later.

It was exasperating. Social Services was up my nose about her, and I was wishing her father would get some sort of a plan together and stop sending her back to me so readily. Instead of a support for him, I had become a crutch he could use as an excuse not to deal with her. My own kids started complaining about things disappearing from around the house – a radio, a calculator, watches, jewellery, money from purses and wallets – always just before she did a flit back to her dad's or wherever it was that she went to.

I was hoping that after she turned sixteen we could get her into some kind of vocational training. I had thought maybe she would be interested in doing a beautician's course since she had such a fascination with makeup. When I mentioned it to her, she seemed to like the idea. But with her, it was hard to know what cheerful enthusiasm meant. Usually it was a smokescreen.

One day I came home to a completely silent house. That was a rare event. I thought it was odd, but also quite delightful. I looked forward to having a cup of tea in the peace and quiet before the after-school bedlam broke loose.

I walked into the kitchen and saw that one of the gas burners was on. I couldn't believe it. I snapped it off and made a mental note to give the entire household an earful for that one. Then I saw something odd out of the corner of my eye. Just on the other side of the kitchen table, I could see what looked like a pile of clothes on the floor.

I walked around and found Susan lying there, face down, with one arm resting near her forehead. My first thought was that she had been at Hughie's whiskey (again!) and really overdone it this time. I kept hiding it in different places to keep it away from her. It was a big disappointment to think my latest hiding place had been discovered so easily.

I put the kettle on and prepared to make her a strong cup of coffee.

I stood over her and called her name a few times. 'Come on now, Susan. You need to get up.' I bent down and shook her shoulder. 'Come on, now, we'll have a cuppa and get you upstairs for a proper lie-down.'

Something about the way her shoulder wobbled seemed wrong. I called her name again, grabbed her shoulder and turned her over. Her face was a horrible pale greenish hue; her eyes were open and glassy.

I screamed, fell down beside her, grabbed her wrist and patted her face. 'Susan! Susan!' I was shouting. Her face felt cold, her wrist had no pulse. My stomach curdled and for a moment I couldn't stand. Everything around me was swallowed in a darkness that had nothing to do with lack of light.

I forced myself up and called for an ambulance, then immediately rang Doris. All I could tell her was that I had found Susan on the floor – and that it did not look good.

She and the ambulance arrived almost simultaneously.

It's too painful, even now, to dwell on the details of that time. But I can tell you that Susan was pronounced dead, right there in my kitchen. They could have hit my heart with a hammer and it would not have hurt me more.

The next day a doctor at the hospital explained to me that Susan had died of a drug overdose. I had to ask him what that meant. I was racking my brain for the drugs we would have had around the house – did they mean aspirin or cough medicine?

The doctor looked at me as if I was either mad or trying something on. He explained that it was heroin.

I just blinked. I had heard about heroin, of course. To me it was something from the movies. I had never heard of people in Dublin having anything to do with it. In some ways, yes, I was naïve. But heroin was definitely not commonly used in Ireland at that time.

Afterwards, I was able to put all the pieces together. The 'wrong sort' she had started messing about with after her mother had died had introduced her to drugs and got her hooked on heroin. The stealing she did was all about getting the money to buy it. The sneaking out late was also about the drug – she was prostituting herself for money to buy it. And whenever she ran back to Finglas, it wasn't because she was missing her dad: it was because that was where she had a ready supplier. It also turned out that her father knew about the heroin. Perhaps he didn't want to face it – or didn't know how to. And perhaps he believed that I wouldn't have helped Susan if I had known about her addiction. But to find out that he had known about her drug use – and that he knew why she was stealing and running away but had never told me – well, it seemed a particularly cruel betrayal. Of both me and Susan.

I felt like the most colossal failure and the most gullible

fool in the world. At the time, and over the years since, people have said to me that there is nothing you can do to help addicts who don't want to get clean. They are self-destructive, single-minded and won't respond – or be grateful – when you try to do anything for them. I suppose that must be true. But all I knew was that a young girl had lost her mother, and some perversity from the bottom of the human heap had offered her a needle instead of solace. I thought anyone could be saved by love and concern. It was the first – but not the last – time that I would be confronted by someone who would reject help and choose self-destruction.

So, I learned that there were people like that. People who would rather lose themselves than accept love and support. But I never learned not to feel their loss as a personal failure on my part.

10

My childhood friend Nan was in the hospital. Hers had been a hard life. Abandoned by her husband, a sickly child to take care of on her own, keeping ends met with a demanding load of work at the street markets, she had a full plate, all right. Now she had heart problems, too. I went to visit her and was delighted to see her sister Tess there. She and I had a great chat, reliving some of our childhood adventures, while Nan rested.

The news for Nan was good: the doctors were happy with how she was doing and she was out of danger. When visiting hours were over, I said goodbye and headed out of a side entrance of the hospital towards the car park.

Just outside the door I saw a man and a woman having a very loud argument. The woman had a child in her arms, and beside her was a small wheelchair. The child had wispy, thin hair and at first I couldn't tell if it was a boy or a girl.

Just as I had gone through the door and was about to pass them, the man grabbed the woman by the arm. He yanked at her violently, shouting the whole time, and I was afraid the child would tumble out of her arms and down the steps.

I stopped and looked at the pair of them. The yelling would have been bad enough. But when it started getting physical, there was no way for me to keep my nose out. Doris would be giving out to me about this one.

I had hoped that when I stopped to look at them, the fact that they had attracted my notice would be enough to embarrass them into silence. Not a chance. The man, a red-faced, sweaty, beefy sort with a receding hairline, kept screaming at the woman. The child was crying now, too.

'You're not bringing a cripple to my house!' the man was shouting at her. 'I'm not having it! Not in my house!'

The woman was yelling right back at him: 'She's your own daughter! How can you just call her a cripple?'

This wasn't a back-and-forth conversation: this was two people shouting continuously at each other, neither of them listening to what the other was saying or seeming too concerned about the wailing child. I got the impression that this was a debate that had been going on for some time. Each knew the other's position and each was refusing to budge. Apparently they had decided to settle it based on pure cussed endurance and decibels. Meanwhile the frail little girl was going to end up deaf if she didn't fall down the stairs first.

The man still held onto the woman's arm and was shaking it and pulling her around. If I didn't do something soon, there would be a royal disaster. Later Doris remarked that it was usually when I *did* do something that we had a royal disaster. Well, then, it would be a disaster either way. I stepped between them and put my hand on the man's arm.

'Let's hold on there a minute.' I managed to help the woman stabilize her grip on the little girl. 'Why don't we settle here a minute and see if we can't get this sorted without all the carrying on?'

'And why don't you mind your own business and piss off?'

Well, he was rude, but at least he let go of his wife's arm. Unfortunately it gave him the chance to turn all of his angry attention on me.

'You need to piss off back to wherever you came from. This has nothing to do with you. Now clear off!'

I had him shouting this into my face, the mother yelling back at him ('Leave her alone! Stop being such a rude bastard!'), and the child was still wailing. I wasn't sure where this ordeal was heading, but I was pretty sure I would be hearing-impaired by the end of it. 'Just hold on for a minute, the pair of you.'

This had no positive effect whatsoever.

'Don't tell me to hold on, you nosy bitch.'

'Jesus, Brendan, would you just calm yourself?'

'Don't tell me to calm myself!' He was livid now. He clearly wanted to grab her and shake her, but I stood my ground between them and he vented his energy by taking a sloppy kick at the small wheelchair. 'I told you I won't be having a cripple in my house and that's the end of it! You march right back in there and tell the bleeding nurses and doctors what done this that *they* can take care of her.'

The poor woman was crying, clutching the little girl, who had given up sobbing and was whimpering with her face buried in her mother's shoulder, little fists glued to her eyes. The mother was still talking, almost a murmur now, as if the shouting had exhausted her. I could hear something to the effect of 'You know I can't do that', 'She's your own daughter, for heaven's sake' and other similar sentiments. He continued shouting and screaming, and I was afraid that he was going to get physical again. I also entertained the faint hope that he would burst a blood vessel and do us all a favour.

'All right now, it's obvious we have a problem between the two of you, so how's about we sit down and talk it out and see what we can sort?'

'I'm not sorting anything with you, you nosy little –'

'Brendan! Enough.'

The eruption had terrified the little girl, who wailed even louder.

This time I was the one who got physical. I grabbed the woman's elbow and steered her away. Over my shoulder, I said to Brendan the Red, 'You stay here for a minute while we get the little one settled down.'

'Settle her down wherever you want, but it won't be at my house!' He shot his wife a filthy look. 'I'm going to the car and I'm leaving in ten minutes. And she,' he stabbed a finger towards the child, 'is not coming with us!'

He stormed off, on thick-soled shoes, I noticed. Trying to look taller than he was, I suppose.

I turned my full attention to the mother. 'So what's this all about?'

She looked at me uncomfortably, lips clamped tight.

'Listen,' I said, lowering my voice. 'I really don't mean to interfere, but I've got a good deal of experience with children of all sorts and I only want to help, if you'll let me. That poor child looks to me like she's suffered enough without all of this carrying-on.'

She was holding firm to her daughter, but her arms

were shaking. She seemed to debate whether to tell me anything, and then when she decided she would, well, it came out in a flood.

Little Jeannie was four years old and had caught a nasty chest infection. Her mum, Sheila, had taken her to the doctor a couple of times and the infection just didn't seem to be getting better. Then, one night, Jeannie had developed a raging fever. Whatever Sheila did, her temperature would not come down. When Jeannie started to slip into unconsciousness, Sheila called an ambulance.

At the hospital, Jeannie had all sorts of evaluations. Alarmingly, this change in her health didn't seem to have anything to do with the chest infection. After a long, long night and a day, during which Jeannie's life was very touch-and-go, she started to respond to her treatment. Not a treatment for pneumonia – a treatment for spinal meningitis.

Jeannie's parents were baffled. Sheila rang their family doctor from the hospital and got a surprising response from his office. He was out sick. He was, in fact, in hospital. He had been there for a couple of days with meningitis. Poor little Jeannie had visited him for treatment of one illness only to be exposed to another.

Meningitis is a dangerous, potentially deadly, disease that every parent fears – but it is also normally very rare. Although it can be awful enough for a teenager or an adult, for a small child the effects can be devastating. Jeannie had lived but the damage to her nervous system had been thorough. Her little legs were weak and almost useless. And I now became aware that her arms were also weak and her hands were always curled in those little clenched fists.

After I had listened to her story, I had to ask Sheila what was going on with her husband.

'I don't exactly know.' She sniffed and shook her head. 'But ever since they told us that Jeannie might never walk again, he's been like this. He won't have her. He just won't have her like this.'

I was in no mood to try to uncover the psychological issues that had made Jeannie's father into a bigoted ass. Perhaps that was what he always had been and no one had ever had reason to notice it before. Perhaps it was just the shock of the sudden turn of events. Perhaps with time to adjust to his 'new' daughter, he would come around. According to Sheila, they had three older children at home and he had always been a fair and caring – if rather strict and demanding – father to them. The way he was behaving today was a side of him she was not used to seeing and she was having difficulty coping. He had no previous history of harming anyone, but based on what I had seen, I did not think it was safe to ignore his ranting and send Jeannie home. I had already seen him get alarmingly close to physical violence. It looked to me as if these people needed a cooling-off period.

'Look here,' I said to Sheila. 'You just need to give him time to get used to the idea. Why don't you let Jeannie come and stay with me for a few days and then, when he's got himself all sorted, Jeannie can go home?'

I explained to Sheila that I had a houseful of kids and had worked with Social Services to get kids off the streets, the whole palaver. She finally agreed. I rummaged around in my handbag and found a pencil and paper. I gave her my address and phone number and she gave me hers.

While this was going on, Brendan had started his car and was flashing his lights at us. This convinced me that I really didn't like him.

With contact information exchanged, I took Jeannie in my arms and Sheila loaded the folded-up wheelchair into my boot. She gave Jeannie a hug, she and I had a quick hug as well, and she went home with Brendan while I headed home with just what I needed – one more child. I have no idea what she said to Brendan. I wonder if he even cared. He made no effort to discuss the situation with me, but drove off, leaving his daughter behind with a complete stranger. That, to him, was a better alternative than taking her to her own home. I will never understand how someone could do that.

When I tell people this story nowadays, they look at me as if I have feet coming out of the top of my head. It seems implausible, unlikely, irresponsible and pretty damn crazy.

A woman turned over her child to a stranger with nothing more than an address and a phone number? Yes, she did. I realize that would never happen today. But forty years ago, in Ireland, such a thing was still possible.

I'm all in support of the laws, rules and regulations that we have in place these days to protect children. But I'll tell you one thing. With the way things are today, if someone saw a couple having such an argument in public, no one would stop and do anything. Oh, they might slink off and call Social Services. Or maybe the police. But no one would feel they could step in and do anything right then and there. People are afraid now to stick their noses in when they see people in trouble. They might get sued. They might get 'involved'. They might embarrass themselves, God forbid. And, equally, many people would be afraid to take any help from someone they don't know because we tend to assume all strangers are potential monsters. So we don't offer help and we don't accept it. That's the fine state of affairs we're in today. I wonder how many children suffer as a result.

But back then I saw no reason not to do something and Sheila saw no reason not to trust me. Seemed like a perfect solution to us both.

So Jeannie came home with me with surprisingly little fuss. The first night she missed her mammy a lot, as you can imagine. I had her in a cot in the bedroom with me and we left a night light on for her. But things got easier after that.

Hughie spent a great deal of time making the ground floor of the house as wheelchair-friendly as possible. This was my first experience of caring for a handicapped child and I had a lot to learn. Older children can reach down, turn the wheels and propel themselves around, but Jeannie was too small for that. Also, her arms and hands were very weak. In many ways, it was like having a very large baby to take care of because she could do so little for herself. But we started a physical therapy programme of our own devising, based on no knowledge whatsoever except a basic instinct regarding what we thought might work.

To me, the basics were to get her out of her chair as much as possible and persuade her to use those weak muscles of hers.

A day went by. Then three. Then a week. I was starting to get a little nervous. Certainly a week seemed enough time for Brendan to have calmed down and come to terms with the reality of his daughter's condition.

After a week and a half had passed, I rang the number Sheila had given me. No answer.

One of the main reasons I decided not to panic was that Doris had insisted, when I told her what I'd done, that Jeannie's parents were freeloaders who had foisted a child they didn't want on me and I would never see or hear from them again. I was, once more, a gullible softy who would end up with another mouth to feed. I didn't believe that was the case – and I especially didn't believe that I ever wanted to hear Doris say, 'I told you so.' At least, not this time.

I had to trust my instincts, and my instincts had told me that Sheila wanted and loved her daughter and would do whatever she had to do to make her husband come around.

Every few days I would ring the number. I continued to get no answer at first. Then someone picked up the phone and said, 'Hello.' It might have been Sheila. When I said, 'Hello, Sheila, is that you? This is Rio,' I heard a click, then the dialling tone. I was in a bit of a sweat by this point.

There was nothing else for it: I had the address so I had to drive over there and see what was going on. I packed up all of Jeannie's belongings and her little wheelchair and

brought her along with me to find her home. I was thinking that the sight of her might prompt her parents into
taking her back straight away.

I found the house in a decent part of Kimmage and
parked the car. With Jeannie in my arms, I knocked on the
door. When it opened, it was herself standing there and
the look on her face, at the sight of me, was not one of
joy. The same facial expression would have been achieved,
I think, if some very unpleasant substance had just
attached itself to her shoes. Instead of inviting us in, she
came rocketing out of the door and shut it behind her.
'Jesus, what are you doing here?'

Jeannie had recognized her mum, of course, and was
squirming to get out of my arms and was making quite a
fuss. Sheila took her into her arms and gave her loads of
kisses, but still managed to look at me as if I had lost the
plot.

'I did try and ring you.' I was a bit baffled as to why I
was feeling on the defensive.

'I know, I know. But it still isn't a good time to bring her
back.'

Oh dear.

'Well, it's nearly two months now. Is her daddy not
missing her? No sign of him softening up?'

She shook her head very firmly. 'Not a jot. Please can
you keep her a bit longer?'

Jeannie was no trouble for me: that was not the issue.
But I could not understand why the mother was letting
the father behave in that way. I was trying to imagine what
would have happened to my own husband if he had tried

to bar one of our own children – or even one of the children not our own! – from the house. Fortunately for him, he never had to find out. What was Sheila's problem? As Doris would remind me later, not all wives are like me with regard to who has the say-so about certain things. More's the pity.

Sheila was clearly terrified her husband would find out that Jeannie had been back, so we said a rather painful goodbye and returned to my car. Jeannie was upset and there was not much I could do to explain to her, in a way that made sense to a four-year-old, why we were leaving her mammy again.

The good news is that Doris never got a chance to say, 'I told you so,' because, in the long run, Jeannie's parents weren't complete freeloaders. Her mother started to come over and visit Jeannie every week, then nearly every day. She had kept in contact with her doctor and the hospital, and Jeannie started some regular therapy. Happily, Sheila became involved in that as well.

When Jeannie had progressed to where she was out of the wheelchair and able to get around with a walking frame, Sheila convinced her husband to let her come home.

It was a happy day for everyone. But my offer to take her 'for a few days' had lasted for nearly a year.

So Doris never said, 'I told you so.' But she gave me an earful of a whole lot of other things I didn't want to hear.

11

Back in those days, things were very tense in Northern Ireland. Even those of us living in the Republic couldn't escape it. We tried to keep our noses out but, of course, the Troubles affected both sides of the border.

I was personally involved in a lot of things happening on the Northern side – but my interests were more to do with trading and driving lorries. Still, with the way things were, everything you did seemed to have political repercussions in one way or another.

For some reason that I have never understood, and probably never will, in the 1970s the government of the Republic of Ireland decided to tax the bejesus out of dairy products – especially butter.

When life gives you lemons, you can use them to make lemonade – or you can get yourself a truck, drive over the border and get cheap, tax-free butter. It became a popular Sunday excursion for some folks to pop over the border, tootle around, buy a carload of butter, then head home and sell it to friends and family for a modest profit. There were those of us with a bit more enterprise who would bring the stuff back by the van- and lorry-load and sell it on for a very healthy profit. Life handed Doris and me buttermilk and we churned it into a huge supplement to our income.

It wasn't long, of course, before the border officials on

the southern side copped on. They hovered like a cloud of irritated bees ready to swarm all over us and make us pay their taxes – or be arrested for avoiding them. And every time they figured out where we were getting across, we would find another way to get our golden cargo over the line – tax free. It's the kind of cat-and-mouse game I love. And what do the government types expect? When they create a challenge, resourceful people will rise to meet it.

Over time, it became a sort of generally accepted method of making a few extra bob. I knew what the strict letter of the law was, but it was difficult to consider the buying and selling of butter as the purview of hardened criminals. So it was not a total surprise when, on one of my trips with Doris, we were at our 'supplier's' location (a small dairy farm in County Down) and met there none other than a priest buying butter to take south.

We were making a large run: Doris was driving the lorry and I was in a van. The lorry was ours, of course, and the van belonged to some friends on the Northern side who were also interested in making some extra cash.

Doris and I were loading up, chatting with our friends at the dairy and getting ready to head out. The priest had loaded his boxes into the back of his van, but was shaking like a leaf and had sweat pouring off him. I guessed that this was not due to an aberrant case of malaria.

I approached him as he was stacking his last box. 'Hey there, Father.'

He nearly jumped out of his skin. 'Ah, hello.' Fortunately, small women with curly hair and glasses aren't generally very intimidating. He relaxed a bit.

'Everything all right?'

He wrung his hands as if worrying an invisible rosary. 'Ah, yes, I think so. So far it's all going well.'

'You eat a lot of butter down in your parish?'

'Ah, now, you know how it is.' This made him really nervous.

'Of course I do. You just don't seem like the smuggling type, if you don't mind my saying so, Father.'

'Well, I wouldn't be, now. But my church is in dire need of a new roof and it has been left to me to raise the money. We've been doing everything possible – but I can't be squeezing blood out of a turnip now, can I? So one of my parishioners suggested this.' He waved towards the butter. Then he pulled at his collar nervously. 'It sounded easy. But now I'm here, I confess that I'm petrified about crossing back over the border.'

'Surely they won't bother a man of the cloth!'

'Oh, now, they will, they will. I'll need to be very careful, I'd say. So I've been given directions on a good way to go, but I'm still quite nervous about the whole thing.' He pulled a handkerchief out of his pocket and wiped his dripping forehead. 'I've half a mind to call it quits. It's just too nerve-racking. And if I got caught what would my diocese do? The more I think about it, the more I think this was a very bad idea.'

'Nonsense.' I patted his shoulder. 'You've come this far. Look at that van, Father – that's your new roof sitting in there! Follow myself and Doris and we'll get you safely to the other side and over.'

His troubled expression changed to one of . . . well, I

wouldn't say happiness, but certainly it was less troubled. We arranged ourselves into a sort of convoy, Doris leading the way in the lorry, me driving the white van that belonged to my friends in Antrim, and Father Bledsoe in his battered green van, carrying the hopes, dreams and the soon-to-be-non-permeable roof of his church, behind me.

We headed south.

After just a couple of miles down the meandering track that would get us over the border, well away from the noses of any interested parties, I looked in my rear-view mirror.

There was no sign of the green van.

I slowed down a bit to give him a chance to catch up.

Still no sign of him.

I slowed some more.

Still nothing.

Shit.

The lorry was well away in front of me.

We didn't have mobile phones in those days. I was stuck with no way to let Doris know what I was doing.

I pulled into the verge as far as I could and waited.

And waited.

Jesus, it was five long minutes before the poky little green van finally showed up. The panicked priest nearly drove into me, though at the speed he was going it would have been barely noticeable.

I hopped out of the van and went to his window.

As he rolled it down I could see he was still sweating and his hands were shaking.

Saints preserve us, I thought. Although, to be fair, since he was a priest, the saints should already have been on board. 'Father, you need to keep up now. We can't be dawdling along here.'

'Oh, sorry, sorry. I just don't want to be caught for speeding.'

I had to blink and take that in for a second. 'Speeding? Speeding is the least of your worries, Father, if you don't mind my saying so.'

He looked at me goggle-eyed. The poor fella was just too rattled to think clearly. That was plain.

'All right now. I'll start again and you need to keep right up behind me.' I peered at him over the top of my glasses. 'I promise I won't drive fast.'

He nodded gratefully. 'Very good, very good – thank you for that.'

Just as I headed back to my van I heard a grinding sound. There was Doris, backing her lorry to get to where my van was parked.

I ran over to talk to her. She was decidedly unhappy. 'What are the two of you doing? We need to keep moving.'

'I know, I know – but yer man there is panicked and won't drive fast.'

'Fast? My granny drives faster than he does.'

'Your granny is dead!'

'Exactly. And she still has him beat.'

'Look, I told him he needs to keep up. I'm going to drive slower and he'll be fine.'

Doris popped her lorry into gear. 'The three of us toddling along at a snail's pace will be a disaster. I'm going on – if you two can't keep up, you're on your own. You know the way.'

I stepped back from her door. 'Fair enough. I'll see you over there.'

The gears ground a bit and then she was away.

I waved at Father Bledsoe, got back into my van, and away we went.

'Away' being a rather euphemistic term for our timid advance towards the border.

No matter how slowly I went, he seemed to go slower. I kept looking in the rear-view mirror, trying to keep him in sight, and he would constantly fall back till I had to come to a near standstill to wait for him to catch up. I suppose his knees were shaking so badly he couldn't keep his foot on the accelerator.

Doris was long gone before us.

It was up to me to drag the quaking would-be smuggler safely across the border and past the Customs officials lurking on the other side.

There were no markings on the little track we were using, so Father Bledsoe couldn't tell when we had crossed into the Republic. But it would have been of little consolation to him – we wouldn't be safe until we were about ten miles into the South, well past the Customs station in Dundalk.

Once we turned off the track and onto something more like a real road, I thought the priest's panic would leave him and we could drive at a more respectable pace.

I was wrong.

He continued to dawdle, like a sloth lounging in a tub of low-temperature marmalade.

I kept having to resist applying some decent pressure to the accelerator and it was making my leg ache. I had to spend as much time looking in the rear-view mirror to see if the priest was behind me as I did looking through the windscreen, and I was getting a crick in my neck. And, of course, Doris was long gone so I would be on my own for the rest of the trip. All in all, it was not the best of times.

I gently applied the brakes again, and around the corner, behind me, I saw the green nose of Father Bledsoe's van creeping forward.

Finally.

We seemed to be inching our way down the road, and this was worrying, as there was now traffic coming from the other side. It wouldn't be long before someone was behind us and they would be irritated by two cars worming their way sluggishly along curvy stretches of the road where they could not be overtaken. I was starting to sweat a little myself.

If we had gone just another two miles, we would have made it to the nearest village and been swallowed into the normal traffic. But out where we were, on a quiet road that didn't go to much of anywhere, two vans crawling along, like a couple of pensioners on rusty roller skates, was just too obvious. They swooped on us out of nowhere – and had likely been following us for a while.

I think they nabbed us primarily because they were sick to death of the bloody creepy-crawling. I could just imagine the two Customs men in their surveillance van saying, 'Bugger this, I want to arrest someone before my teeth fall out . . .'

At any rate, the next thing we knew there were sirens, a garda van and some Customs cars. Poor Father Bledsoe (who amazingly did not piss himself) and I, with our vans of 'contraband', were hauled off to the Customs depot outside Dundalk.

We were asked why we had so much butter.

They directed their questions at Father Bledsoe. Apparently, he looked like a ringleader and I was a mere accomplice. I decided to let them find out for themselves that the poor man couldn't have led a Ring-a-ring o'roses.

Father Bledsoe did not disappoint.

'All right now, Father, do you mean to say that this one hundred and sixty pounds of butter in the van you were driving was for your personal consumption?'

The priest's eyes were bulging and his collar was soaked with sweat. 'Grrrgggh,' was all he managed.

One of the Customs men, whom I thought of as Frog Face, acted as though that was an intelligent answer. Perhaps, in his range of experience, it was. 'Now, Father,' he said, and crossed his arms. 'That seems like an awful lot of butter for one person, all at one time, don't you think?'

Poor Father Bledsoe. Everything he had feared had come to pass. All he could think about was the trouble he was going to be in with his diocese. He was thinking that being caught as a smuggler was going to mean the end of his tenure at his parish, the end of any hopes he had for advancing in the Church – it might even mean the end of being a priest. His whole life was crumbling before his eyes and these interrogators wanted to ask him about how much butter he ate.

He appeared to give the entire situation a great deal of consideration, mopped his brow (again) and replied, 'Blrrrrrgllll.'

Then he started to weep.

Frog Face was a hard man. I expect making priests cry was all in a day's work for him. He turned to me. 'So.'

I blinked back at him. There was a long silence.

He tried again. 'So.'

He was expecting the awkward silence to make me blurt something. I was blurtless.

He tried another tactic. He stood up and started pacing around the room. The other Customs man, the Mouse, remained seated – and silent.

'One hundred and sixty pounds of butter in the green van, and two hundred and twenty in the white van.' He leaned over his desk and glared at me. 'Do you have a tax receipt for any of it?'

Father Bledsoe blew his nose into his sweaty handker-chief. Frog Face turned his glare in the priest's direction. 'Well? Any receipts?'

I was afraid that the priest would clear all the snot out of his head and say something intelligible – and incrimi-nating – so I decided to speak up. 'Don't we get to make a phone call?'

Frog Face was not happy. He looked at the Mouse, who shrugged and nodded.

'Yeah, yeah – you get to make a phone call.'

'I think we can make some calls and get this all straight-ened up.' I leaned over to the father. 'Isn't there someone in your parish you would like to call?' I grabbed his wrist so he would look at me. 'Someone who knows you're here?'

I was hoping he would take the hint that he should call whoever it was who had helped him organize coming up to collect the butter: perhaps they might be helpful in extricating him from this mess. Otherwise I was afraid he would panic and do something useless, like phone his bishop and tell him everything. This was no time for confessions – of any kind.

Meanwhile, I made a call of my own. The Customs men were listening, so I had to be careful. I suppose they thought I was calling for legal help, or for someone to bail me out if it came to that. But I called my friends in the North who owned the van I was driving. 'Hello, this is Rio . . . Yes, my friend the priest and I were driving our vans – the white one and a green one – and got pulled into the Customs station here at Dundalk . . . Yes, it would be great if you could come down here and help get it sorted. Thanks.'

I hung up and smiled at Frog Face. 'They said they'll be here in an hour.'

'To do what?'

'To get it all sorted.' I smiled again and asked if I could get a cup of tea for the priest.

Frog Face and the Mouse decided they were happy enough to let us stew for an hour. They might get proof that the taxes had been paid, or more likely they would be able to book us, confiscate the butter and charge us a huge fine. Either way, things were looking good for them.

Meanwhile, I also knew that before too long things

(*Left*) The five of us with my father, Joseph O'Reilly. Baby Joseph is on his knee and, from left to right, Anna, Frances, me and Colette. (*Right*) I'm about five here. The picture was taken in our garden.

(*Left*) The whole family at our summer house – Colette, me, my mother (Winifred), Anna, my father with Joseph and Frances. (*Right*) Me and Hughie during our courting days.

Our wedding day in 1959. Hughie's sister Betty made my beautiful dress.

Me and Hughie outside the little dress-making shop I ran with his sister.

My great friend Doris, who died so young, with a child I was fostering.

In full flow in the Waterford Apple Market. I had just been to the hairdresser, so the plastic bag was there to protect my 'do'!

My parents lived to a ripe old age. I'm to my father's right as he cradles a baby I was fostering. To my mother's left my daughter, Gwen, is holding her daughter, Nicola. The other two little girls are my son, Patrick's, daughters, Susan and Nessa.

After a wedding in the late 1990s, with three of my four siblings: Colette (*left*), me, Joe and Frances. Anna lives in Australia and wasn't able to attend.

It's wonderful to see each generation of the family growing up. The above picture shows four generations: me (*left*) with my mother and my daughter, Gwen, at her daughter, Nicola's, christening. In the picture below Gwen is the granny and I'm the great-granny to Nicola's (*left*) baby daughter, Kourtney.

The People of the Year Awards in 2010 was an unforgettable, special night. I'm with Gwen on the left and Patrick, Hughie and James (one of my foster children) on the right. (*Below*) With Frances Fitzgerald (now Minister for Children), Aidan Waterstone, senior social worker and long-time friend, Catherine McGuinness, former Supreme Court judge, and then Fianna Fáil minister Mary Hanafin.

Hughie and I at a party to mark our fiftieth wedding anniversary. (*Left*) I still love to get out and sing a song or tell a story. Here I am in full flow a few years ago in the Cellar Bar in the Dunboyne Castle Hotel.

With my great-granddaughter, Kourtney.

'My happy, secure, if somewhat eccentric childhood had left me unprepared for a world in which a child could be unloved, unwanted and uncared for.

Even when such situations were staring in me in the face, I always believed that these were temporary lapses brought on by circumstance.

For the most part, I still try to believe that.'

would definitely get sorted one way or another. My friends who owned the van were very possessive. And they wanted their van back. With the butter.

An hour went by.

The Mouse and Frog Face had dumped the priest and me in a busy room full of desks and phones and people running about. We were plonked on a couple of wooden chairs against a wall with lukewarm weak tea in plastic cups and left to wait. We were waiting for salvation, each in our own way.

He had found his rosary beads and murmured over them between noisy bouts of nose blowing. He was too distraught to talk to me. I never found out who he had called. And I did not want to tell him that I was getting things sorted for both of us. There were too many other ears around, and I wasn't sure what was going to happen.

After the hour had come and gone, Frog Face came in to check on us.

'Where are the people who are supposed to sort this out?' Frog Face still thought that the priest and I were partners in crime, so he directed his glare at the father.

An hour of nose blowing had not helped his nerves. A confrontation with the uniformed man sent him into an emotional tailspin. 'Plrrrrgnnn?' was the best he could do.

Frog Face turned his glare on me.

'Sure these things take time. They'll be along soon.' I smiled at him. 'Might be they got caught in traffic.'

No doubt that made Frog Face concerned that who-ever was coming along to help was the same sort of driver as the priest. In which case, we would all be there till Christmas.

'They'd better get here soon or the two of you will be spending the night in a cell,' he snarled, and left us to our tea.

Another hour went by and I could see the Mouse and Frog Face conferring in the hallway, looking through the glass in the door to where Father Bledsoe and I were sitting. Frog Face was agitated. The Mouse was ominously quiet and would stare at us with unblinking brown eyes.

Frog Face had just put his hand on the door handle and was about to come in, probably to drag us off to the dungeons, when there was an incredible uproar throughout the building. A siren was wailing somewhere outside and a slew of people came tearing through the hallway. Someone in a uniform ran up to Frog Face and yelled a lot of unintelligible things with big arm gestures and the two of them raced off. Phones were ringing and people in the room were walking quickly in and out, back and forth. Others were dashing to the windows, looking and pointing.

Eventually they were turning to take furtive looks at myself and the priest. They did not seem happy.

When the tumult finally died down, it was the Mouse who came to see us. He stood in front of us for a moment, arms folded, staring. 'Come with me.'

He turned and left the room. Father Bledsoe and I followed him. The poor priest had such trembly knees they were practically knocking together as we went down the hallway back to the room where we had been interrogated. Frog Face was already there.

When he closed the door behind us I knew we were in trouble.

'Okay, you smartarses, where are they?' he thundered, his bulbous froggy eyes threatening to pop right out of their sockets.

'Glllbrrrbb!' Father Bledsoe collapsed into a chair in a heap.

'You!' Frog Face came right at me with a finger stabbing into my face. 'Who did you call?'

Like I was going to tell *him*. 'What's this all about?' I turned away from him and looked at the Mouse.

He kept his oval brown eyes in an unblinking, rodent stare. 'We have a bit of a problem.' At least he was remaining calm.

'Is it your problem or my problem?'

Frog Face nearly leaped over his desk. 'Don't you be a wise-arse with me!'

I kept my eyes on the Mouse.

The corners of his mouth, where his bristly whiskers should have been, crinkled into a rueful smile. He shrugged.

'Where are the damned vans?' Frog Face had grabbed Father Bledsoe by the front of his shirt and was shaking him. It caused a new eruption of gurgles. And snot.

'Leave him alone! We've been sitting in here for two and a half hours. How would we know where you put our vans?'

'Ah-heh-hrrrm.' That was the Mouse clearing his throat. He gave Frog Face a look that would have curdled milk. Or perhaps melted butter.

Frog Face let go of the priest. 'We don't have your vans.' He almost mumbled it.

'You what?'

He slammed his hand on his desk. 'We don't –' SLAM '– have –' SLAM '– your fucking vans!' SLAM.

'Whaaarrrllp?' Father Bledsoe had perked up a bit.

The Mouse scratched behind his ear. He used a finger, but I bet when he was alone he used a hind paw.

'Some uniformed men entered the car park and left with your vans.' He scratched again. 'We now have reason to believe they were not actually . . . ah . . . hrrm . . . officials of the Customs Department.'

'Are you telling me that my van, and the van that belongs to the father here, have been stolen from a government Customs office car park?'

Now it was Frog Face's turn. 'Eh . . . yeh . . . lllpp.'

'This is outrageous.' I wanted to dance a jig around the room. In a feat worthy of a golden statue, I kept the expression on my face stern.

'It certainly is.' The Mouse had a cold anger about him.

'Well, what happens to us now? Are you going to press charges or what?'

The Mouse really bristled at that. 'No, obviously we can't. We have no . . . evidence.'

'So we are free to go?'

'Yes.' The Mouse looked at me very strangely. 'You can both go.'

Frog Face slumped into the chair behind the desk and thumped a fist on it. But he had nothing to say.

'Come on, Father. Let's call a taxi and go home.'

The Mouse stuck out his hand. 'Oh, no. No taxis for you. You can walk.'

Walk! We were bloody miles from civilization and another phone. Dundalk town was well beyond walking distance.

'But we need to get this man back to his parish.'

The whiskerless Mouse twitched again. 'That's unfortunate. But, given the security concerns we have here, it's the best we can do.'

Frog Face punched the desk again. 'Just be glad you're getting outta here at all. If it were up to me we'd skin the likes of you alive. Now get out.'

No need to ask me twice. I pulled the priest to his feet and we walked out.

'Luuuurf!' Father Bledsoe raised his hands and his eyes as if to thank Heaven for his deliverance.

I knew better.

A few hours later, after we'd managed to get a lift to help us on our way, we were meandering up a winding track, back the way we had come earlier in the day, and reached what looked like a cow path. We stopped at a half fallen-down barn behind a stand of trees.

There were the vans.

Father Bledsoe had back his van and butter intact, along with a map showing him a way to get home that went nowhere near Dundalk. Meanwhile, my load of butter had been transferred into a red saloon car. The white van would stay in the barn for a while, until the Customs folk stopped looking for it.

My partner in crime drove away, map in hand, and I never heard from him again.

My friend handed me the keys to the red saloon car with a wink. 'Better luck this trip, Rio!'

Well, I could certainly find my way home, if I didn't have any further interruptions . . .

Eventually, the impact of events in the North became inescapable. Hundreds of men and women were rounded up by the government on suspicion of being members of the paramilitary. Through some kind of legal wrangling, they managed to incarcerate them, then hold them without trial. No one was able to tell how long they would be held, or if they would ever be let go. Meanwhile, many of them had children who were now left with one parent (who couldn't afford to feed them, with the main wage earner being locked up) or no parents at all. Hundreds of families were in absolute tatters.

The churches, various folk and organizations tried to find ways to get the kids sorted, but they quickly became overloaded and had to look outside their own borders for help. Father Neary and I had already got to know each other well, dealing with the French boys. I guess I shouldn't have been surprised when the knock on the door turned out to be himself.

'Well, Father, come in. Have a sit-down and a cuppa.'

'Thank you, Rio, I will.'

When he sat down he had the coiled look of a spring that would unleash itself at the slightest nudge. I knew the way he operated – he would sit there and make small-talk, work his way around to the subject, then finally ease me into whatever it was he wanted me to help with. I normally enjoy the social niceties as much as anyone. But then again there are days when I just want to get to the bloody point. 'What is it, Father? Something up?'

One of the dogs was already sitting on his feet. He scratched her behind the ears and looked up at me – a faint smile, but not one with any laughter in it. 'You have the right of it, Rio. I need to ask your help. We have a few children from the North who need somewhere to stay for a few days.'

'Well, that's not a bother, you know that. What ages are they?'

'We're not completely sure – anywhere from toddlers to teenagers.'

I nodded. 'Well, we can cope with that around here. Sure I've got beds for another three. I could take five if I get the kids to double up.'

He looked up at me and I saw that he was really tense now. 'It will be a few more than five, Rio, I'm sorry to say. I know it's a lot to ask but we need you to take in a half-dozen – maybe ten.'

I don't know it for a fact, but I think the expression on my face must have resembled that of a constipated guppy.

It made him panic a bit.

'It's just for a day or two! Then we'll get them sorted to various homes where they can stay longer term if need be. But we need to get them out of the North, Rio. Between the parents being in internment and the stress these kids have been under with all the violence, we just need to get them out now.'

'You do know I have only a three-bedroom house?'

'I do. I know it will be a stretch.'

A stretch? I felt like reminding him that I wasn't the one who could feed the hungry masses with a stale loaf and a few scrawny fishes.

He wouldn't give up, I had to give him credit. 'It's just for a day or two. These kids need a bed and a hot meal while we get the rest of it sorted, that's all.'

I looked around my kitchen, plotting where I could set up extra beds, wondering who would let me borrow some pillows and blankets, deciding how I could rotate a dozen kids through one bathroom.

My distracted look made Father Neary think I was trying to find a way to back out. He stood to go. 'Well, it's a lot to ask, I know. Thanks, anyway.'

'Hold your horses, Father.'

I picked up a piece of paper and a pencil from where the kids had been doing homework at the kitchen table. 'Now, tell me what's what.'

I called Doris and had her gather up as many blankets, pillows and towels as our friends and family could spare. She brought them over in the van. She had also brought some bottles of milk, boxes of cereal and loaves of bread. Bless her, she had called in favours from all over. We unloaded everything and the house seemed filled to bursting. And we didn't even have any of the kids yet.

'Jesus.' Doris was looking around the kitchen and into the hallway. 'I just can't see where you're going to put everyone.'

'Well, me and Hughie can sleep on the floor. And we'll

put some cots out in the lounge. We'll have to feed them in shifts.'

'Of course a couple will come to my place.' I hadn't asked her to do that – she wasn't as keen on having strangers in her home as I was. For her, that was a particularly big move.

'Well, there you go. That will be a big help right there.' I felt better already.

The next afternoon we had things ready and we waited for their arrival.

And we waited.

And then we waited some more.

I phoned Father Neary once, but got no answer. So there was nothing we could do but continue to wait.

Fortunately it was still the part of the summer where the sun went down very late, or we would have had to deal with it in the pitch black – but at nearly ten o'clock at night, hours after we had been expecting them, the first car arrived with four kids. Right behind it, in a convoy that ribboned down the street, more cars came. And more. And even bloody more. What the hell?

Father Neary popped out of one of the cars and came in to help put some order in the mish-mash of people that were pouring through the doorway.

So far I had seen ten children crossing my threshold. And the cars kept arriving.

The priest was tired and dishevelled. He pulled me aside. 'Listen. I'm afraid there are a few more children than we thought. Things are very tough up there.'

Kids were still filing in. Bloody hell – I'd counted thirteen.

I gulped. 'All right so. How many are we talking about?'

He fumbled with a piece of paper he pulled out of his coat pocket. 'Em . . . *twirtle-feeve* . . .' he mumbled pathetically.

'What? How many did you say?'

He cleared his throat. 'Now, we'd been expecting about a dozen, as you know, but then the cars just kept showing up.'

Out of the corner of my eye I counted at least four more children. Doris was directing the flow like a traffic warden.

'And?'

'Em . . . we have thirty-five. Altogether. Total.' At least he had the decency to look embarrassed.

'Jesus wept!' That was Doris. She made no apology to the priest for her outburst and, fair play to him, he didn't seem offended.

'All right so.' The children, some of them carrying small bags, others a blanket, a few with nothing at all, kept coming in. My own children were standing on the stairs, occasionally yelling helpful directions. 'That's it! Put your bag on the table or the dog will get in it!'

'Where do we start?' Doris was trying to get everyone into one place – some of them had wandered into the back garden.

'Two things,' I said. 'Gwen and Rose, get your blankets. You'll be sleeping in the bath tub. Father, you and I need to go up and down the street and knock on some doors. We'll never get all this lot in here. We need some help.'

So that's what we did. I went to every single one of my neighbours and, God love them, at eleven o'clock at night, out of the clear blue, some of them opened their doors and found room for one or two. By the time we got back to my place, I had only to scrounge enough room for fifteen.

You do remember Father Neary saying that it would be just a day or two, right? A load of you-know-what, yet again. I had them for more than a week. They were aged two to seventeen, some were siblings, some were alone and so frightened I don't know how they got through it. But somehow, all of us, we managed.

Meals were done in shifts of six at a time. Even with all those hands to help, I was heartily sick of peeling potatoes! The washing-machine ran constantly – but first we had to make sure that everyone labelled their clothes and their towels, if they had their own. We still had an occasional kerfuffle when someone decided they liked someone else's blouse better than their own. (If the government up in the North was really serious about ending 'hostilities', they should have sent a platoon of teenage girls to sort it: very little can stand up to that level of viciousness.) We set up a chart with a rota of chores on it – for dishes, sweeping, taking out rubbish, minding younger ones, walking the dogs, and on and on. One of the kids cheerfully (I hope!) nicknamed the place 'Camp Rio'.

Over the next week and a half, one by one, or two by two, Father Neary managed to find places for them. It was a relief and a disappointment at the same time – I found the house too quiet after they were all gone. The hustle and bustle had been exhausting but also exhilarating.

I never again had that many children all at one time. But, sad to say, that was only the beginning of the influx of internment children. Over the next three years, I would continue to take them in, never more than a handful at a time, and serve as a sort of intermediary until either the Church or some other agency could find them something more permanent.

A lot of things I learned at that time stood me in good stead later: putting name tags on the clothes; making rotas for housework and homework. They turned out to be good ways of keeping things running smoothly even when it wasn't like trying to organize a small army. As any mother can tell you, trying to manage three or four kids can sometimes seem like a job for a field marshal.

13

After the big crowd from the North were no longer in the house, things got back to what passed for normal at my place. Of course, it didn't last long.

My son Patrick once told me that he would leave the house in the morning to head off to school and wonder how many kids would be there when he came home. He looked forward to there being someone new – and always hoped he'd have a lad of his own age to pal up with.

I think I must have let him down in that regard because he decided to bring home one of his own.

Patrick had been friends with his classmate, Charlie, for years, and I was used to seeing him around. One day after school, Patrick asked if Charlie could stay for tea and, of course, I said yes.

Teatime came and went, and Charlie was still with us. Next thing I knew, I was asked if Charlie could stay the night – even though there was school the next day.

Well, this seemed eerily familiar.

The next day after school, Charlie came home with Patrick again – and he had brought a bundle of clothes with him.

I pulled Patrick aside. 'What's all this about?'

'Oh, Charlie needs to stay here again tonight. I told him

it was okay.' And with that he ran upstairs to help his friend get settled.

I was touched that my son had just assumed that Charlie would be welcome, and that it had never occurred to him that I might say no. When I told Doris about the new visitor, she said I was touched all right.

Well, I could understand that occasionally fourteen-year-old boys have a hard time at home. That is an age when a lot of rows with parents, or fights with brothers or sisters, can erupt, or when there's just some need for breathing room. I could understand that he might need to get away for a few days.

But every day I saw another bundle come into the door with him, every day he seemed to get more settled, and Patrick was unfazed about sharing his room. A week went by.

I finally asked Charlie, 'Does your mother know where you are?'

He shrugged in a noncommittal way that was not at all reassuring. 'Yeah, I guess so.'

Guess so? I had a vision of his aggrieved mother storming through my front door, accusing me of holding her son captive. Something here did not smell right, and I'm not talking about the usual malodours to be expected from fourteen-year-old boys.

The next afternoon I drove the couple of miles to Charlie's neighbourhood. I knew where he lived, but I couldn't say I knew his mother well.

I knocked on the door.

She answered, holding a potato and a small knife. When

she saw me her eyebrows shot up and tried to escape into her hairline.

'Rio! It's you, isn't it? Is everything all right? Is Charlie okay?'

That was a classic case of good news/bad news. Good: she knew where Charlie was. Bad: she knew where Charlie was and it didn't seem to bother her much.

'Well, yes, he's fine.'

'Oh, thank goodness. I was afraid he'd done something wrong and you were going to send him back.'

I definitely felt on the wrong foot now. She had made no move to invite me in and seemed entirely too comfortable with the idea that her son was staying with me.

I knew a thing or two about kids who were big trouble – and Charlie was not one of them. I couldn't understand why she was so easy at having him out of the house. 'Well, of course he's welcome to stay with us, but I wanted to make sure you weren't expecting him to come back.'

She looked panicked at the mere thought. 'Not at all, Rio. I was hoping you could keep him for a bit. There's just no room for him or Peter at the moment.'

'Ah, so you're all right with him being at my place, then.' This seemed like an understatement.

She put a hand on her heart, the hand with the small knife in it. 'Oh, absolutely. You gave me a fright there. I thought you'd come to tell me he'd acted up or something and that you wouldn't be able to keep him.'

This was the first time I understood how the other women in my area thought of me: I was running some sort of youth hostel, apparently.

I stood there for several more minutes while she explained to me what was going on. It was a cold, blustery day and I was freezing. I didn't need to come in and be offered a Sunday dinner on her best china but a step inside out of the elements would have been nice. No chance. She just stood there, holding her door open wide enough to tell me her excuses.

At any rate, it turned out that the poor woman had fifteen children. Three of the oldest ones had gone off to England a few years earlier for work, and just in time, too: it made enough room for the younger children. But something had gone wrong over there and now two were back. The house was ridiculously overcrowded. They had been short of beds to begin with, and with the two big ones back home, there wasn't even enough floor space.

I don't know why – and I didn't ask – the older ones stayed and it was the two youngest who were forced out. And she had encouraged them to go elsewhere. Charlie, obviously, had landed with me. His brother Peter was staying with a friend in Ballyfermot.

Later, when I was explaining this situation to Doris, she snorted and blew a belligerent cloud of smoke across my kitchen table. 'Some women shouldn't have kids. Especially when they don't have any more sense than that.'

'I agree. Thank goodness the two lads had somewhere to go.'

She folded her arms and still managed to point her cigarette at me. 'Everyone is playing you for a sucker, that's for sure. "Oh, I can't raise my own children – I'll send them off to Rio. She'll keep them for ever."'

'Tosh.' I opened the kitchen window to get some of that smoke out. 'Charlie will only be here till summer. Then the older lads will find some work, be out of her hair, and he can go home.'

'And I'll learn to play the piano with my arse.' She smirked. 'You just watch. You'll end up with this one, just like you've ended up with all the others.'

She was only half right. Which – she later pointed out to me – meant that I was at least half wrong.

Charlie did move out and away from us one day. Mind you, it was after he'd finished school and completed his training as an electrician – when he was nineteen. And his mother never did invite me into her house. Leaving people out on the kerb was, apparently, her speciality.

14

By the mid-1980s, my own kids were grown but still at home, and there were several others as well. Rose and Charlie were still around, and there were occasional drop-ins from the Finglas market. Generally, everything seemed pretty settled.

Not for long, though.

Doris had a neighbour, a woman she had known for years, named Grace, who had three children. Doris and Grace had been very close before all the kids had come along, and Doris had tried to be a sort of aunt to the little ones. Unfortunately Grace was a flighty party girl and she didn't seem too interested in letting Doris get involved with her children. Grace had never been married and her ten-year-old Ben, eight-year-old Tammy and three-year-old Sharon had different fathers. In those days, that was still a bit unusual, but at least she had been allowed to have her children and raise them on her own without having to hide anything from anybody.

But Grace was not one to settle down to mothering very easily. She seemed to be on a constant prowl for the next good time and the next soon-to-be-ex-boyfriend. Doris was convinced that the kids were left alone for long stretches to fend for themselves and this infuriated her.

The more she tried to stick her nose in and 'help', the more Grace kept her away. It was an ugly tug of war.

One particular weekend, the tug seemed to go in Doris's favour.

We all knew Grace had a new boyfriend – a hairy, boot-faced lump who was big on cheap suits and drove a ridiculous, ancient Italian sports car. It was a convertible with a battered, leaky roof and we all thought it was hilarious to have a car like that in Ireland. But Grace thought it was the poshest thing in the world, so what could you do? Lately Grace had been spending more time flitting about, getting her hair blown into a frizzy rat's nest in that leaky vehicle, than she had been at home – and Doris had noticed. When Grace announced that she and her new lover-boy were going off for a weekend to Fota Island, near Cork, Doris wondered aloud who would be minding the kids.

Grace ignored her and kept her travel plans a bit vague, not wanting any interference.

Over the next few days Doris kept ringing her neighbour's place, but got no answer. Finally, late on a Saturday afternoon, she decided to pop over and see what was what. Doris knew there was a chance that Grace might not like being checked on – she might blow up and make a scene. Her behaviour had become erratic over the years, due to alcohol and God knew what else, according to Doris, and two furies like Doris and Grace, head to head, made the D-Day landings in Normandy look like a sedate tea with your spinster auntie.

But there was no blow-up and no big scene. No one

answered the door. Thinking she heard some noises, Doris peeped into a couple of windows. She did not like what she saw.

The next thing, she was in my kitchen, barging around and waving her arms.

'Well, what did you see exactly that's so bloody awful?'

'I saw Ben. He had the telly on, but he wasn't watching it – he had a black bin bag in his hand and was swinging it around all over the place.'

I cocked an eyebrow. 'That doesn't sound too dire.'

'You wouldn't think so – except that little Sharon was in her playpen screaming her face purple. And he just kept swinging it around.'

'Maybe he couldn't hear her over the telly.'

'Bollocks. He could see her well enough. He didn't seem to bloody care.'

'And no sign of Grace?'

Doris shook her head. 'Not a hair of her or Tammy. And I didn't see Boot-face's stupid car there either.'

'Maybe Grace was asleep.'

'With all that racket going on?'

'Okay, passed out, then.'

Doris wrinkled her forehead. 'I suppose. But that doesn't make it any better. Why wouldn't anyone answer the phone when I rang?' She stubbed out her cigarette in a saucer on my table. 'It doesn't smell right and I want to go in there and see what's what. Will you come with me?'

This was a powerful statement about the ferocity of which Grace was capable. There weren't too many situations in which Doris needed reinforcements. She would have strolled onto Omaha Beach by herself and told the Germans to stuff themselves.

'Of course. Let's go and have a look.'

In our woolly jumpers and sensible shoes, we drove over to Grace's terrace house.

First we tried the obvious. We went to the front door and rang the bell. We knocked furiously. Nothing happened. We tried to open the door. No luck there either. We peeped in the front window and saw no sign of anyone. Doris had phoned before we went over and still no one was answering.

We went to the back door and did some more banging. Still nothing.

From the back window we could see past the kitchen and into the rear corner of the lounge, where Sharon's playpen was. I could see a foot and a bit of her back. She was lying down, napping apparently.

Strange, though, that the doorbell and all the knocking and banging didn't seem to bother her.

Doris apparently came to the same conclusion. She was peering over my shoulder and swearing. 'Where's Ben? Or Tammy? If Grace isn't here, who in the hell is minding that baby?'

She grabbed the handle to the back door and started yanking and twisting it. When that didn't work, she kicked it.

I was still looking through the window, and thought it was particularly odd that this commotion was getting no reaction from the little body lying on the floor of the playpen.

'Doris, we need to get in there.'

Doris had her shoulder to the door and was battering it. 'I know.'

'Here, give me a hand.' I was trying to get my knee up on the windowsill. The top part of the window didn't look very tightly latched. In my teens I'd been an expert at getting into and out of my parents' house to beat the curfew so I knew that this was a window I could open.

Doris used her shoulder to boost me up.

'Give me your comb.'

Without a word, she dug into her shoulder bag and pulled out a comb with a long, pointed 'rat tail'. That was the nice thing about being with Doris: I didn't have to explain to her and she didn't need to ask.

I used the long, pointed end of her plastic comb to jimmy the top part of the window open enough to reach in and open the main latch. Then it was up and we were landing in a sink full of nasty, crusty crockery.

I dropped onto the floor and went straight to the playpen, with Doris right behind me.

Sharon still didn't move.

This really was not looking good.

I reached over the edge of the playpen. God, the smell was appalling. To say it reeked of dirty nappies wouldn't even be close. Plain old dirty nappies would have been refreshing in comparison. It smelt like something was rotting.

I reached down and touched Sharon's shoulder.

'Sharon, baby, Sharon – are you awake? Can you wake up for me?'

Doris was behind me, speechless for once.

Sharon moved her head a bit, pulled a hand up to her face and just whimpered.

I noticed she was wearing nothing but a filthy T-shirt – not even one of her own: it was huge on her and looked like it belonged to her brother. Beneath that, she was wearing a sagging, soggy, oozing nappy. She was nearly four. Why was she in a nappy? A frayed and unpleasant blanket was twisted around her. It smelt strongly of wee.

'Is she okay?' Doris was trying to reach down to her.

I was closer, so I felt her forehead. It wasn't hot. She didn't have a fever. If anything, it was too cool. Her face was pinched and sunken.

'Well, she's alive but I wouldn't say she's all right. I'd say she's a right mess.'

Doris frowned down at her for a moment, then wheeled away from the playpen.

'BEN! TAMMY!' She went out to the small hallway and yelled up the stairs. 'BEN! If you're here, you'd better get down here NOW! TAMMY, where are you?' I heard stomping as she went up to see if she could find them. For their sakes, I hoped they weren't there.

I looked around the room. It was a cluttered, filthy mess that a family of weasels could have happily burrowed into. Mounds of papers and wrappers gave off the distinctive odour of very old fish and chips. And the place reeked of cigarette smoke. Half-filled ash trays were visible here and there.

I found an old woolly throw that was covering up the majority of the stains on the back of the sofa, wrapped Sharon in it and picked her up. There was a great deal of leakage of things I didn't want to think about from her sagging nappy. I used the throw to keep the worst of it off my coat.

Doris came storming down the stairs. Her face was purple and contorted. Her anger was rapidly approaching meltdown.

'No sign of the bleeding little buggers and of course Grace is long gone. Her makeup and toothbrush aren't here.' She touched Sharon's forehead and looked into her little face. 'You okay there, chicken?'

Sharon stirred a little bit. 'I'm hungry,' she managed to whisper.

I wrapped the throw a little tighter. 'Come on, let's get her out of here. She needs a bath and something to eat.'

We headed for the hallway. Just as Doris was reaching for the handle, we heard a key in the lock and the door swung open. Standing there, with a bag of chips in one hand and a can of fizzy drink in the other, was Ben. He blinked at us. 'Whaddya doing here?'

I thought Doris was going to tear his ears off and stuff them up his nose. She grabbed him by the collar and the chips splattered on the floor.

'Hey, that's me dinner!'

Sharon had started making a noise. It wasn't crying, and it was too loud to be moaning, it was a heartbreaking kind of keening. To me, it sounded like someone too far gone to cry. Whether she was too drained emotionally or too drained physically was hard to tell. But the sound of her brother's voice had made her tremble so hard that my teeth were clattering together.

It was then that he noticed we had Sharon.

'Whaddya do –'

But before he could finish the thought, Doris had throttled him again. 'Where have you been? Where's Tammy? Why did you leave the baby alone?'

He shrugged. 'Tammy's at her friend's place. I went out to get somethin' to eat.' He tipped his head towards his sister. 'She was all right.'

'All right?' Doris shook him again. 'Do you smell that? Does that seem all right to you?'

Ben just shrugged again. He gave off a strong smell of cigarettes. That seemed odd for a ten-year-old boy. He ignored his sister and didn't seem too bothered about us either. The spilled chips seemed to be the only thing that concerned him.

Doris let go of his jacket. 'Where's your ma?'

He smirked. 'She's away. She's been away for days.'

'Days?'

'Yeah. Can I pick up my chips now?'

Doris stared at him.

'What?'

'My chips. Can I get them off the floor?'

Doris was looking at him as if she had never seen him before. Well, to be fair, this was a side of him she never had seen.

Ben took the lapse to be his opportunity, bent over and scooped the chips back into their paper wrapper.

I finally felt I could say something. 'Look, Ben, we're going to take Sharon with us.'

He stood up and popped a chip into his mouth. 'Yeah, all right.'

'If your ma calls, be sure and tell her what we did.'

He walked past us into the living room. I heard him say, 'She won't call,' and then he switched on the TV.

Doris started to go after him. The look in her eyes was not murderous exactly, but it was not kindly either. I grabbed her arm. 'Leave him. We'll deal with him and your friend later. Let's get Sharon out of here.'

Doris nodded. She was fuming and shaking almost as much as poor little Sharon. I could see that the best thing would be to get her away from there.

As we went out of the front door, I turned and called to Ben, 'If you need anything, love, you know Doris is right down the street – you ring her if you need to.'

I could hear the television – it was not loud. I knew he had heard me.

But he didn't answer. So we left.

As we headed down the footpath to my car, I was muttering.

Doris tossed her head. 'What are you saying?'

'That place. It was such a wreck.'

'What of it?'

'I thought you said you saw Ben with a bin bag.'

She looked at me. 'I did. I definitely did.'

'Well, what on bloody earth was he doing? He sure as hell wasn't cleaning up.'

Neither of us had an answer for that.

Back at my place, the first thing we did was commandeer the bathroom and run a nice hot bath. Then it was time to start peeling off the mess that was all over little Sharon. I actually stood her up in a bucket when we removed the nappy and I had to make several attempts at cleaning her before it was even safe to pop her into a tub of water. Safe for the water, that is. While she stood there being swabbed down, I gave her a glass of milk. She drank it so fast I was afraid it would come straight back up. I had Doris make her a small mug of warm milk with honey in it and told her to drink it slowly. It seemed to give her a little strength.

Once we got her in the bathtub and started making some progress with the layers of dirt, Doris and I were able to get an idea of the real state of things. By the time we had her out of the tub and were rubbing her skinny little arms and legs with a soft towel, Doris had to keep looking away so Sharon couldn't see her face. Or the tears that were streaming down.

Sharon was nearly four, but she was the size and weight of a much younger child. Her ribs stuck out of her skin in a way I had only seen in those adverts for starving kids in Africa. Her pinched features and the circles under her eyes told me she was also dehydrated. She had sores on her bottom from wearing a soaked and filthy nappy for so long. She was potty-trained, but from what we could gather, whenever Grace was out, she found it easier to keep the child in nappies. That way she could plop her in her playpen and just leave her. For days on end, apparently.

That would all have been bad enough. But she also had bruises on her back and on her legs. Now, I know that toddlers get bumps and bangs. But there were a lot – and in clusters. Some were old yellow-green ones; others were fresh and starkly purple. And then, here and there, on her arms and ankles, there were small round shiny pinkish marks that told a very different story. Especially the ones that hadn't scarred over yet where you could very clearly see that they were burns. Burns the size and shape of a cigarette end. She had at least a dozen.

After her bath, Sharon had supper with the rest of my children and we put her to bed. She dropped off to sleep very quickly. We came back downstairs. Doris and I stood in the kitchen and looked at each other. Without a word, I went out of the back door into my walled garden. Doris was right behind me. I took a deep breath, then walked over to the bench where I had some small clay pots, all in a row, with marigolds in them. I looked at my garden wall for a minute, then reached down, picked up one of the pots – and threw it as hard as I could against the wall. Without a word, Doris came up next to me and did the same. She screamed as she threw hers. We were both standing there, tears rolling down our faces, staring at the muddy splats on the wall. I like to think that I'm a woman of action, not of violence, but I really think that if Grace had walked into my garden at that moment I would have killed her.

Two days later, Grace came home, all in a lather, wondering what we had done. We braced ourselves, expecting her to raise a rumpus. But she wasn't stupid: she knew she had been caught out. All I had to do was mention the possibility of calling Social Services – not to mention the police – and she backed off. It wasn't safe to have her in the same room with Doris (indeed, it was years before

Doris could be alone in a room with her) but I was able to have several conversations with her, some more coherent than others. The long and the short of it was that Sharon was going to stay with me or I was going to file a report with the authorities. I made it clear to Grace that this was not open for discussion. For once, Doris didn't give me any stick about putting my nose in.

Grace didn't give up Sharon easily, but when I talked to her about the bruises and scars, she became very alarmed. Piecing it all together, a tragic state of affairs emerged. Grace, apparently, had left Sharon regularly in Ben's care. As in almost all of the time. Weekends, after school and, of course, on those 'holidays' she was forever taking with her flavour of the week. Tammy had realized she could make herself scarce and go to a friend's house whenever Ben was left in charge. And Ben did not like being left to babysit all the time so he had developed his own way to cope. This included the beatings and the burns. Yes, it was a ten-year-old boy who had lit the cigarettes and burned his sister with them. He didn't actually smoke them, as far as I know. That Sharon's own mother had not even noticed the abuse and the marks was all the evidence anyone would ever need to know that Sharon had been shame-fully neglected by the woman who had given birth to her.

Over the next few months, Grace made noises about changing things at home so that she could bring Sharon back. Doris and I knew a load of horse manure when we heard it, and we made it clear that that was never going to happen. Time went on, and Grace got carried away with other boyfriends and unsavoury pastimes. Eventually she latched onto some loser and she, Ben and Tammy moved with him to Canada. Sharon stayed with me.

It was just a few days after Sharon arrived that another mystery was solved. She was in the lounge, watching TV with everyone else, and I came in with a black bin bag to clear away some of their clutter. She screamed double bloody murder and jumped behind the couch. I don't know how but her brother must have discovered, when she was very small, that she was terrified of the black sacks. Or, even worse, perhaps he had done something that had made them terrifying. After that, all he had had to do was wave them around to torture her. And that was what he had done, for no other reason than to make her scream.

After the initial fright and heartbreak, Doris and I were pretty happy that we had got Sharon out of that environment while she was still small. We assumed we had saved her. How damaged can you be at three years old, after all?

The depth of her problems became obvious early on. I had her in the park one afternoon, and an acquaintance came along with her infant in a pushchair. After I had admired the new child, we started to chat. The next thing I knew, Sharon had reached into the pushchair, grabbed the baby by the shoulders and was shaking it.

We put a stop to that right away, of course – but it was terrifying. Sharon had gone for that child like a rabid terrier after a rat. It was a horrible thing to see. I had to keep her away from babies after that.

When she started kindergarten we had problems over her interactions with other children. She would slap. She would bite. She would throw intense tantrums. I had to get some help.

When she was six, I took Sharon to therapy. We went through a whole legion of different treatments, doctors, nurses and tutors. She had psychotherapy; she had help with control of her aggression and with her 'learning difficulties'; she had coaching for her social interaction skills. You name it, we got her help for it. I was willing to try anything. The poor child had had a terrible start in life, and I believed she deserved any help we could get her.

She improved, as time passed, but she was never like any other child I reared. She never formed a bond with any of the children in my house. She never seemed to like or trust anyone – not even me. As a teenager, she was a nightmare. Wilful, deceitful, aggressive, selfish. Doris and I tried everything we could think of. Sharon would undermine us every chance she got.

In her twenties she settled down and the worst of it seemed to be over. But she still struggled with depression; she still had difficulties maintaining relationships. Doris would get upset and blame herself for not noticing what was going on earlier. If only we had got her away sooner, she would say, we could have prevented the damage.

Perhaps.

Or perhaps some damage can never be undone, no matter how early you detect it.

Inflicted early enough, with enough severity, some hurts just can't be fixed.

15

By now, Father Neary had walked up the footpath to my door many times. The first had been more than twenty years earlier. Back then he had been a parish priest; now, he had a wider scope of responsibility, working with Social Services to help families all over the west Dublin area. He had been trying his best to pull me further and further into that 'scope' for some time.

This time the door was opened by a lad of about eight. I could hear the pair at the door.

'Hiya, Father.'

'Hello, son. Is she in?'

'Sure she is. Come on in.' He pulled the door open. 'Would you like a lolly? We have more. The red ones are the best.'

'No, thank you, but you're very good to ask.'

He was a kind young fellow, that boy, and obviously thought it was rude to be sucking an ice lolly and not to offer one to the visitor.

He escorted Father Neary into the kitchen. Pots were burbling away on the stove. There were two children at the kitchen table, school books, papers, pencils and crayons scattered about. They were jabbering and flipping pages. Two posters on the wall displayed multiplication tables. Shelves around the room held figurines of angels, faeries and butterflies. More children were outside in the garden, kicking a football. A dog was barking. I'm sure the priest must have thought it was like entering a beehive.

I was at the sink, cleaning a couple of chickens for roasting. I peered up at him over the top of my glasses.

'How are ya there, Father?'

'Very well, Rio, very well. And yourself?'

'Can't complain. Sure you'll have a cuppa tea? Sharon, put the kettle on, will ya? There's a good girl.'

'No, no. I won't be here long. I just need to ask you for something.'

I pulled the chickens out of the sink and placed them in a roasting pan. 'Oh no you don't.' I gave him a grin. 'Look at the state of the place.'

'Of course. But I could use your help all the same.'

I was rubbing the chickens with salt and pepper and looking over at the kitchen table. 'Christine! Don't use your crayons for your homework! Use your pencil.' I turned back to the priest. 'And what is it that I can help you with, Father?'

'It's a family that needs your help – and you'd be helping them and me both. It would be in a sort of formal capacity.'

'Formal?' I snorted. 'Whatever that means.' I placed the roasting pan in the oven and checked the potatoes. 'I can't take in any more children right now, just so's you know.'

'Yes, I understand.' Father Neary had to step to one side as Patrick came tearing through the kitchen and nearly knocked him sideways. 'I want you to help some of the mothers.'

My eyebrows went up as I wiped my hands on a towel. 'The mothers?'

'Yes, I have some families that are struggling and they just need someone like yourself to come in and help them organize their homes. Someone who can help them cope with a houseful of children, the laundry and the school work.' He waved his hand around the kitchen. 'We have some poor mothers that will lose their children to foster care if they don't get a grip on how to deal with things. We're looking for folks such as yourself to come out to them two or three times a week and just help them get organized. We're calling them "visiting home helpers".'

I had to grin at that. 'Now look at me, Father. I'm up to my nose in "homework".'

He smiled. 'Rio, ever since you took on the children from the North I've known that you have a knack for organization. You managed to keep the show on the road then, even though you had children all over the place. It would be great if you could help mothers of big families who aren't coping. I'm dealing with women who have seven, ten, even fifteen kids, and they don't have a clue how to manage. Maybe help them figure out how to plan meals, budget their housekeeping money and organize things for their kids.' He gave me a hopeful smile. 'It's a rare gift to be able to manage – and I've seen you do it.'

I tapped a wooden spoon on the window. 'Put that down! And give him back his shoe!' I turned to Father Neary. 'Well, I can only come in and tell them the things I figured out on the fly. I don't even know if they're right or wrong. I just know that they work for me. Mostly.'

'And that's it exactly. I have a family nearby I'm working with right now. Will you come with me tomorrow for a quick visit to see if there's anything you can do?'

'Sharon, be a good girl and see if those clothes on the line are dry, will you?' I turned to the priest and pushed my glasses up a bit. 'Well, I can pop in for a visit and see if there's anything I can do to help. I can't promise I can do it full-time, like.'

'Oh, no problem – that's grand. I'll collect you at ten in the morning. Will that suit?'

'All right so.'

'I'll see myself out. Thanks a million, Rio. See you tomorrow.' He turned to go.

'Father!'

'Yes?'

'As I said before, I'm not bringing home any more kids!'

'I know. Thanks, Rio.'

The next day, Father Neary collected me and we drove to a treeless area of council flats. The family we were visiting consisted of a mother, father, seven children and an eighth on the way. They were squashed into a flat that was far too small for them. He explained that he was trying to sort out better accommodation for them, but in the meantime, they needed to get their current living situation under some kind of control.

The outside of the building looked like most buildings of the sort: ugly, square architecture. Oddments of rubbish were scattered here and there, bicycles in various states of repair, random piles of dog shit. We climbed the stairs to the second floor.

'This is it.' Father Neary hesitated. 'Em, I guess I should warn you . . .'

'Warn me? You're warning me now when we're on the bleeding doorstep?'

'Sorry, but . . . well, things here are a bit rough. Just remember, that's why they need your help.'

He knocked on the door.

When it opened, I didn't see the girl standing in front of me. I felt as if my head had been buffeted by the plume of stale, wretched air that escaped.

As Father Neary stepped inside, the assault escalated. Little hands grabbed at his legs and arms. He laughed and gave each hand a squeeze. All four children were yelling at the top of their voices. 'Sweets! Where's the sweets?'

He stopped and reached into his coat pocket. 'Why, I just might have some right here.' He stopped for a moment and looked perplexed. 'Oh dear, I hope I didn't forget them.'

There was a flood of moans and groans.

A little boy, who looked to be about five, piped up, 'You better not have forgot, ya poxy bastard.'

I nearly swallowed my teeth. 'Now then, we won't be having that kind of language!' I pointed my fiercest mum-glare at him through my glasses. The tyke responded by kicking me in the shins. 'Jesus!' I reached down and rubbed my leg.

The boy stuck out his tongue at me, shoved one of his smaller siblings out of the way, and grabbed at the priest's arm. 'Ya got any or not?'

Father Neary took a step forward so that they could close the door. 'All right, all right. I was just teasing you, children. Here are some sweets now.' He pulled a handful out of his pocket and held them out. The result was similar to a feeding frenzy I had once seen on a television nature programme about hyenas.

While the children were occupied, I took a look around the room. It was a cramped space, made more cramped by the accumulation of random bits and pieces of unrecognizable junk (there appeared to be pieces of a dismantled car engine sitting in a corner), piles of clothing and blankets that did not look likely to be clean, rumpled sheets of wet newspaper scattered about, and at the end of the room, in the corner, what appeared to be the kitchen. There were chairs and a table, littered with dirty plates and cutlery, crusty pans and other cooking utensils, crumpled bags and wrappings. Some flies were wafting lazily around, others crawling undisturbed across the layers of grease and the carpet of crumbs that served as a table top.

Next to the sagging sofa there was an accumulation of cardboard boxes and dingy, dismally ragged pillows stacked in a crude half-circle. I could see a ginger head of curls behind it. I walked over and found a girl, aged about a year and a half, penned up in the roughly organized containment area. She wore a filthy T-shirt that was too small for her and nothing else. There had been an attempt to cover the small bit of floor beneath her with newspaper. It was wet, shredded in places, and smeared with a greenish brown slime. She was lying on her side, looking towards me. The only noise she made was a wheezing sound, her tiny chest trembling with the exertion of each breath. Her eyes followed me as I moved closer.

Father Neary came up behind me. 'That's Lily, the youngest. She's had some kind of lung condition since she was born. I think I told you there's another on the way.'

'Where's the mother?' I had to clench my jaw to stop myself screaming. My hands were shaking and I half hoped she wasn't there: I might be tempted to tear her head off if I got within two feet of her.

The priest turned to the girl who had opened the door. 'Would you get your mammy?'

She furrowed her brow and pushed her hair behind her ears. Her younger brothers and sisters were scrabbling around on the floor for a sweet that someone thought they might have dropped. 'Mammy's resting. She doesn't like to be bothered when she's resting.'

'It's okay, love.' I tried to smile. It was like trying to swim through plaster. 'She'll want to see the father now, won't she?'

The girl didn't seem sure, but she ran towards the back of the flat, knocked on a door and slipped inside the room.

The priest turned to me. 'It may take her a few minutes to get up and come out here.'

'Well, then, I'll have a good look around, shall I? Get an idea of what needs to be done.'

I had already determined that there were no nappies for the little ones – that was why there was newspaper all over the floor. I poked my head round a door to the left of the front room and found a bathroom – there was no hot water at the tap. The smell had been a fair warning, but I decided to be thorough and lifted the toilet lid. It was backed up with solid matter that gave off a reek to choke the devil. I dropped the lid, gagged and immediately ran my hands under the cold water in the sink. I looked for soap. Or a towel. There was just the ubiquitous newspaper. And some soiled clothing, even dirty dishes.

In the kitchen, I poked around in the presses, hoping to find food. There was a box of Weetabix with little more than crumbs at the bottom. Some grubby plastic cups, a box of teabags. And several small bottles of vodka. There were hard crusty piles of dark matter scattered here and there on the shelves. Mouse droppings, probably.

The fridge was a tiny thing on the floor, stuck crookedly into a corner. I opened it and was greeted by a waft of warm, swampy air that smelt of fungus. The boy who had kicked me was behind me. 'That don't work.'

'Yes, I see that.'

'We keeps the milk and butter in the sink. Ya can put cold water on it, see.'

He went to the sink and pulled up a small bottle of milk that was just a quarter full.

I took it from his small hands. It was tepid. I looked in the sink and the only thing there, floating in a puddle of water, was a small plastic tub of margarine.

'That's very good – thanks for showing me. Is it all right if I look at a few more things around here?'

The boy shrugged and started to pick his nose, but continued to watch me carefully.

I poked through the piles of dishes and pots, and opened another press, below the sink. This was apparently where they had been putting their rubbish. There was a plastic pail that had been filled with food scraps, dirty newspaper, food wrappers and empty tins. It was roiling with a lively population of maggots.

I slammed the door shut.

When I straightened, I leaned on the sink and closed my eyes, squeezing my mouth closed so that the children would not see me fighting the bile rising in my throat.

I heard footsteps and voices behind me. I didn't know what to expect when I turned around – I didn't know what kind of demon the woman in charge of this household would turn out to be. A huge, vicious, alcoholic with rotten teeth perhaps. Or a shrill, demanding harridan with a wicked temper. But anyone who raised a family in this manner must surely be a decayed husk of misplaced humanity.

I turned and saw Father Neary beside a small, fragile woman, with a bird-like delicacy of bone and movement. Her once-blonde hair was a drab greyish yellow, pulled back in an elastic band. Her pregnant belly looked like a disfigurement, a grotesque growth completely out of proportion to her frailty. Her face was youngish, near to forty, but her eyes were lined with an age that had nothing to do with years. She moved hesitantly. The children crowded around her and she held out a hand to ward them off. 'Don't knock me over! Who's watching Lily?' Her voice was surprisingly strong and rough, an incongruous mismatch with her slender lightness.

The kids all babbled at once, and the eldest one made a beeline for the stack of pillows that served as Lily's playpen. Her bed, too, most likely.

'Rio, this is Maddy, mother of this brood.'

I put out my hand. 'Nice to meet ya.'

Maddy didn't smile. She didn't seem surly or unfriendly. She seemed numb.

'Well, yas can all sit down.' And she sat down herself in a chair furthest from the window.

I kept quiet as Father Neary and Maddy discussed things; I kept my eyes on the kids at times, on Maddy at others, listening, taking in the story of how this family had come to be, as the story fleshed itself out.

The father was rarely at home, but he was around. He seemed to be the sort who was always dabbling in money-making notions, such as engine repair, but wouldn't stay sober or interested long enough for anything to pan out. The dole money seemed to disappear like breath on a glass and they were always short of everything. Maddy couldn't answer for where the money went: she didn't see much of it. She suspected he did some betting as well as drinking, but would never dream of confronting him. It seemed to take all of her energy to ask for milk money for the children.

Because Maddy was not feeling well with this pregnancy, the kids were not going to school regularly – there were many mornings when she just couldn't get up. The two youngest children, Lily and a boy of three, hadn't been potty-trained. The toilet only worked occasionally and Maddy had run out of the stamina and concentration needed to train the kids to do more than aim for the ever-present newspaper. Mealtimes were random, sometimes missed; shopping was chaotic.

Everything in the household reeked of abandonment. Maddy had abandoned all hope of exerting any control over her choices, her surroundings or the trajectory of her life. The father was both the abandoner and the abandoned – adrift in a miasma of drink, aimlessness and unfocused rage. The children bore the brunt of the abandonment, eking out an existence in which they were half starved of love and sustenance.

I felt ridiculous. How could the priest have thought I could come in here with my shopping lists and laundry rota and homework schedule and make any kind of difference to their lives? I had never felt so overwhelmed. For the first time in my life, I felt totally inadequate.

When our visit was over, Father Neary and I said our goodbyes. A couple of the children had gone outside; the rest clung to the priest as he was trying to leave. They begged for more sweets, they begged for a cruise around the neighbourhood in his car, they begged to be taken down to the shop, they begged, they begged, they begged. Maddy sat, dry-eyed and unsmiling, on the chair where they left her, her hand on her distended belly, clenched in a white-knuckled fist.

The fresh air outside the door slapped me in the face. I shuddered with the cold delight of it, shaking off the fug of what we had left behind. Yet the parting had torn at me. How can I leave them here? I thought. And how will I ever be able to come back?

We walked down the flights of stairs in silence. Halfway down, my stomach got the better of me: I lurched to the railing and surrendered to the clawing nausea that had been stalking me for what seemed like hours. I staggered back and Father Neary patted my shoulder. 'I know, I know,' he was murmuring. 'It's very difficult, breaks the heart . . . I know.'

I pulled a tissue from my pocket and dabbed at my lips. Tears were dripping down my cheeks. 'Jesus, Mary and Joseph!' I glared at him over the top of my glasses. 'Pardon my language, Father, but what in the name of Heaven have you got me into?'

His smile was tired. 'I wonder myself, Rio. This is all new territory. We'll have to figure it out as we go, I'm afraid.'

We continued down the stairs. The drive home was fairly short; I was unusually quiet. Father Neary tried to get me to talk about it – he explained the plans he had for helping families like Maddy's; he had told her that the home helpers would do so much more than the Church and the charities had ever been able to. But I could not be drawn into a conversation.

After we stopped in my drive, I sat for a moment. 'What do we do next, Father?'

'Ah, so you want to help, do you? That's great to hear.'

'There is nothing in this world I would rather *not* do. But you know as well as I do that I can't just walk away from it. So where do I start?'

'Could you come along tomorrow? Yourself and another home helper can get them started on cleaning the place. I'll be sorting some things with a social worker.'

'Fair enough. I can do that.' I opened the door and got

out. Before I pushed the car door shut, I turned to him. 'But I won't be bringing home any more children. Is that clear? I won't be having any social workers or this one and that one putting their noses into my business.'

He nodded. 'I understand. Anything you can do to help is very much appreciated, you know that.'

'All right.' I shut the door.

Over the next few weeks, I made several trips to the flat, with another home helper named Helen. We spent hours sorting through rubbish, showing the kids how to sweep and dust and mop, scrubbing floors and toilets, sinks and dishes. Laundry had to be dealt with. Shopping lists had to be worked out. A schedule for getting the kids up and off to school was arranged.

But, through it all, Maddy stayed distant and uninterested, the father nearly invisible – except to burst in and throw a tantrum.

We found a used playpen for Lily, and I tried to get Maddy involved in bathing and playing with her. The toddler had been struggling with lung problems since she was born and was supposed to be taking medication. A social worker and a home nurse sorted that out, so I helped train Maddy in how to give Lily her medicine and the breathing therapy that she needed. But even this failed to engage her: Maddy remained distant and removed.

For me, the sessions with Lily were the only part of the visit where I felt I had accomplished something. At first Lily had been a scarily quiet child, but as the days passed, she got more energetic, more playful. She said only a few words, but it was clear she was bright enough to learn more. She needed time, I knew. Time to heal, time to get stronger. But the nurse had warned me that if the medication wasn't given regularly and if the therapy didn't progress, time would be limited. Maddy seemed unable, or unwilling, to help Lily fight for her little life. I had to do all the fighting, and it was wearing me down.

On many days, Helen and I would arrive and Maddy would stay in bed. Everything that we got sorted would be undone either by the children, who slipped back into their chaotic ways as soon as they were left alone, or by their father, drunk and belligerent, determined to get the priest and the home helpers out of his way.

The nurse came once a week to check on Maddy's pregnancy. Maddy was meant to be taking vitamins and getting out of bed more. Instead, she seemed to be slipping further and further into a world consisting of her darkened room and a cocoon of musty blankets. It was the only space she cared to inhabit. She did not eat; she did not tolerate, let alone enjoy, the company of any of her children. We were losing her.

It was very early in the morning when my doorbell rang. I was already up. In my dressing-gown and slippers, I had been getting out bread and ham for the children to make their sandwiches to take to school. I opened the door, expecting the bin man or some such, not Father Neary. His face looked grey, the lines around his mouth deeper. 'Jesus, Father, you're a fright! Begging your pardon. Now do come in.'

He came into the hall and stopped. 'Rio, can you get

away and come to Maddy's? Someone needs to stay with the children for a bit.'

'Well, of course. What's happened?'

'The baby.'

'Ah, Jesus. Oh, sorry again, Father. The poor dear is early!'

Before Father Neary could answer, I was putting on my coat and calling up the stairs: 'Sharon! Come down here, love, I need your help.' I turned back to the priest. 'Now, let me get my handbag . . . My goodness, I'm not ready for this at all. She's at the hospital, I take it?'

'Yes . . . She's not well, I'm afraid.'

He had given this kind of news before. He waited.

'Oh, no! What's wrong?'

Father Neary heard some footsteps upstairs. He had to make this quick. 'She wandered off last night in that storm – they found her this morning, racked with a fever. She lost the baby.'

That day there should have been rain. It seemed to me that the heavens should have been pouring, though whether to mourn or to purge, I wasn't sure. At the least there should have been grey skies. The emptiness above our heads should have been dark, oppressive and bleak. The crystal blueness and optimistic sunshine of that winter day was breaking my heart.

Father Neary's car drove through the busy streets towards Maddy's flat, and I blinked at the bright blur of colours as people flitted about, doing all of the mundane things of their lives as usual. If only, I thought. If only we could go back to life as usual.

When we arrived, a social worker and a nurse were there. The children were in the front room, oddly subdued. Voices rose and fell from the bedroom at the back. I couldn't make out what they were saying, but it seemed to be the usual roaring of Maddy's husband punctuated by the temperate voice of another social worker. She was trying to stem the flood of his drunken denial. And drowning.

Father Neary and the social worker immediately went into a huddle, she with a fistful of papers. I went to the children. Two of the smaller ones got up, let me sit down on the crowded sofa, and climbed onto my lap. Ah. Life as usual.

I had to blink for a moment and force a smile. 'So, has everyone had some breakfast? Do ya need anything?'

There was some mumbling, some nodding.

I looked around the crowded floor. 'Where is Lily?'

'A nurse has her. She was wheezing again. Didja bring any sweets?'

I tousled the nearest head. 'Just could be that I did, love. How about if we look in my bag?'

There was so much milling about.

The social workers and Father Neary were filling in papers, a policeman came and went, the nurse was popping around, to and fro. The children's father made an appearance, refused to sign something, made a fuss, upset everyone. He disappeared, then came back – more amenable after having had a few pints. He finally did whatever it was they wanted him to do, but made sure he was surly about it. He left in an uproar, slamming the door behind him. He had never even looked at the children.

I had to make several trips getting kids to the toilet, fetching glasses of water, making cups of tea, finding a lost shoe. But, compared to what else was going on, it seemed as if the children and I stayed still while the milling went on around us.

Finally, it was time. Father Neary had tried to prepare me, but there was nothing for it except to let it happen. He explained to the children that they would be going to foster homes. Three were going to one home, and three to another.

At first they just looked at him as if he had spoken Greek. They had no idea what a foster home was.

'You're going to live with other families for a while.' I hoped that I sounded cheerful. I was trying so hard.

The eldest girl had copped on first. 'But why? Why can't we stay with our own ma?'

'Now, you know she's in the hospital. This is just until she's well enough for you to come home again.'

'Bollocks!' That was the five-year-old. 'I doesn't want to go nowhere.'

Father Neary stooped down to look the youngest ones in the eyes. 'I know this seems a bit scary – but you'll be somewhere where you get lots to eat and have your own bed and everything.'

As these were all things completely out of their experience, they just looked back at him blankly. One little girl hiccuped.

'And you can all come and visit me whenever you like.' I nearly bit my own tongue off when I realized what I'd said. But there it was. I had said it.

A couple of the older children smiled a bit at that. The younger ones still didn't know what to think.

Their belongings were gathered, coats and hats found, a sort of order was imposed and the social worker got them ready to take them to their new homes.

I hugged each of them goodbye, gave each a sweet, kept my eyes dry for their sakes.

Then they were gone. An entire family of children, dispersed like so many loaves of bread. But only six of them.

'Where is Lily?'

Father Neary looked as tired as I had ever seen him. 'She's still in the bedroom with the nurse.'

'Why didn't she go to a home with some of her brothers and sisters?'

He sat down. He was shaking a bit. 'She can't go to a foster home, Rio. We don't have any foster parents who are prepared to take in a child with such a serious illness. She'll go to an orphanage.'

It was a relief finally to have somewhere to spend my anger. It came with a volcanic urgency. 'An orphanage for that poor little thing? After all this family has been through? She bloody well will *not* go to an orphanage. Over my bleeding dead body!'

I didn't care that I was talking to a priest. A stream of language that I normally reserved for bad drivers and corrupt politicians thundered out of my mouth as I stormed back to the bedroom. The nurse had laid Lily on the bed, on her side, where she lay pathetically still, her chest rising and falling with soft wheezing sounds. The nurse was sorting through her medications – a small satchel was already packed, with her few clothes and a ragged pillow that she liked.

When I walked in Lily lifted her head a little and smiled, reached out a hand. I leaned down and picked her up, my grip gentle but firm.

The nurse turned to me, but said nothing. Father Neary came through the door directly behind me. 'Now, Rio – you know it's best. No one knows better than yourself the amount of help this child needs.'

'That's the first smart thing you've said! She certainly needs better than she'll get in some bloody orphanage. She needs more than medicine and therapy and you know it – this child needs *care*. Real honest to God *care*.'

I realized now that my face was wet and my glasses were slipping. I had held the tears back for so long – it seemed for ever. The torrent had started.

Father Neary stepped closer. 'Rio, she either goes into the foster-care programme with someone who can care for her or she goes to the orphanage. There are no other choices.'

I glared at him – the effect ruined by the globs of tears, and my need to give a big sniff.

The nurse came up to me, arms out, as if to take Lily away.

I felt the rattling in Lily's chest as I held her close. I looked down and saw the small mouth curl slightly upwards in a smile, the lips tinged blue. Lily's brown eyes gazed back at me, earnest and unblinking.

'All right, give me your papers and I'll fill them in.' I turned to the nurse and gave her the full force of my over-the-top-of-the-glasses glare. 'And you give me that damned satchel.'

I shifted Lily to my shoulder and patted her back. 'I'm taking this child home.'

16

So, by the early 1990s, I was official. I had been roped into working with the Health Board as a home helper. It seems odd, after all the years I had spent bringing children into my home, that Lily was the first 'official' one, a true 'foster' child.

Not all of the children in foster care needed full-time homes. Sometimes they just needed to be in a place for a few weeks due to some temporary problems at home – mother in the hospital, or father in jail, that sort of thing. And then they went home. Sometimes a foster parent just needed a break. They would ask another foster parent to keep a child in their care temporarily. I had helped out with many of these 'short-timers'. So when I was asked to keep seven-year-old Trevor for a couple of weeks, it wasn't a bother at all.

Though the social worker did warn me: Trevor had been abandoned for the most part, left alone for long periods of time, and was malnourished when he was first taken away from his mother at the age of two and a half. He had subsequently spent time in several different foster homes and then been put into a residential home for little boys run by an order of nuns and had lived there till he was six.

Then he had gone back into the foster-care system, but

even though his new foster parents offered him a caring family environment and tried very hard, Trevor had proved to be more than they could handle. Not too surprisingly, given his difficult childhood, he had a lot of behavioural problems, including not being completely toilet-trained. After the first home, he was shuffled around from place to place. It seemed no one would keep him for more than a few months. His current foster family had found him very 'trying' and had asked for a couple of weeks away from him as a break.

At the time, I already had a houseful and was not in a position to take another child full-time. I had Lily, Sharon, four-year-old twin girls (Katie and Juliet) that I was fostering, and another couple of children who were staying short term. But taking one more for just a short break? No problem.

So some time in October Trevor came to stay with us for 'a couple of weeks'. We tried to get him settled into a routine with us. Like many kids, he didn't particularly like school and every morning he put up a fuss. Mind you, his fuss was something terrible, but I knew a thing or two about abused children by now. I actually believed that there wasn't anything he could do that would surprise me.

Things went fairly well at first. He was not a friendly child and he very much stuck to himself. Well, that was not unexpected. The poor little fella had been through a lot in his short life.

But his temper. Holy Jesus! That kid could fly off the handle faster and more furiously than anyone else I had ever seen. And I spent a lot of time with Doris! And you never knew what would set him off. When Trevor blew up, it was a full-fledged, mindless tantrum. Kicking, screaming, throwing things, lashing out at whoever was nearby, tearing things to bits. Chairs, lamps and dishes were broken. People were scratched, bitten, kicked and pummelled. Even the older kids became terrified of him. What made it so difficult was that you never knew what would set him off – it seemed very random. You might bump his elbow at the table, or someone might have moved his book bag. Or another child had more chicken than he did on their dinner plate. It was hard to avoid setting him off when you weren't sure what would do it.

After one extreme outburst, in which I nearly lost half of my dining set and a couple of kitchen chairs, I sent him up to his room to cool off. Later in the evening, after I had managed to get him to go to bed, I sneaked into his room and brushed back the hair on his forehead to see if '666' had been carved there by the devil. I couldn't wait for the two weeks to be over.

Then the two weeks was past and still no word from his foster family. I rang the social worker and asked what was going on.

The family were still recuperating: could we keep him another week or two? I said yes, but I was thinking, I'd better stock up on holy water.

One day I was cleaning the family bathroom and found some soiled underpants wrapped in a plastic bag in the wastebin. By the size of them, I knew they belonged to Trevor.

That day, when he got home from school, I took him

aside and showed him the plastic bag. 'Trevor, love, why are you throwing your underpants away?'

The look of terror on that little boy's face was heart-breaking. This was part of the reason I felt compelled to help him, I guess, rather than just give up on him because of his ranting and raving. Sometimes he was terrifying, all right, but at other times he was clearly the one who was terrified. And just as his temper could be baffling, it could be difficult to understand the things that seemed to scare the hell out of him. The knowledge that I had found his soiled underpants was one of those terrifying things and I certainly hadn't meant to frighten him.

His eyes filled with tears and he started to shake. He tried to talk but I couldn't understand what he was saying.

I touched his shoulder. 'Now, now, love, it's okay. I'm not angry.'

He looked at me as if he didn't believe it. He cringed, as if expecting to be hit.

'Trevor, everybody has accidents sometimes. It's not a bother to me one bit.'

He was still looking at me like he didn't believe it, his shoulders shaking with the effort of holding in his sobs.

'Look here.' I took him by the hand and we went into the utility room. 'Here's a bucket I keep by the washing-machine. Any time you have an accident, you just bring your undies down here and rinse them out in the sink, like this.'

I took his pants out of the plastic bag and showed him how to rinse them under the tap, then put them in the bucket and add a little more water so that they could soak.

He watched me silently, sniffing back tears.

'You see? This will be your bucket. And that way,' I leaned towards him as if we were sharing a secret, 'we don't have to throw away any of your underwear because that would be very dear, wouldn't it?'

He seemed to consider this, then nodded.

'So there you go. This will be your bucket. And, Trevor . . .'

He looked up at me, probably expecting the blow to land, I suppose. But all I said was, 'And no one else needs to know.'

He gazed at me very solemnly and nodded again. For him, that was almost a smile.

So, he had clearly been terrorized and punished and made ashamed of his 'accidents' in the past. Rather than face that with me, he had tried to hide it. At least now he knew that in my house he would never be punished for any such thing.

After that he was healed and everything was great, right?

Not a chance.

The tantrums continued and the other children were complaining about things 'disappearing'. Bags of crisps, sandwiches, sweets, fruit – all sorts of items would disappear from the table, the fridge, their lunch boxes. I thought they were imagining things. But one day I did a thorough clean of the room that the boys were sharing: behind and under Trevor's bed and in his dresser I found mounds of wrappers and crumbs and crusts and orange peel and even food that had never been unwrapped and eaten. Sharon used to do the same thing, to a lesser degree, when she was little. I had learned that this was typical behaviour for kids who had been malnourished and underfed. I cleared it up, but I never mentioned it to him. What would I say? 'I know you nearly starved to death once, but please stop worrying about food'? I decided the best way to get him to stop would be to let him get used to having enough to eat. And that would take time. Perhaps he had been punished for taking food to his room and that was why he had to 'steal' it and hide it.

It occurred to me that all of the 'terrible' behaviour in his life might not be entirely coming from Trevor. Perhaps some terrible things had been done to him well after he had been removed from his mother and that 'unsafe' environment.

This theory was pretty well confirmed when more weeks went by, and the next thing I knew, his foster family asked if we would mind keeping him through the holidays. These people had clearly given up on him. I advised the social worker that I would keep Trevor for now, but that she would need to find a new permanent home for him after the New Year.

Meanwhile I struggled to control his erratic behaviour. Once he locked a child in the bathroom. Another time, I found him out in the garden. He had persuaded one of the other children to climb on to the shed roof and was shouting, 'Jump! Jump!' He was not convinced when I explained to him that jumping from a height of twelve feet was not good for anybody.

One night we had Brussels sprouts at dinner and this helped to clarify things. Trevor ate his just fine, but one of the other kids decided she didn't like them. When she left hers on her plate and we were clearing the table, Trevor got hysterical. 'You've got to eat your sprouts! You've got to eat those!'

At first we thought it was funny – I actually thought he might be making a joke, which would have been a first.

But then he grabbed her by the arm and was screaming. 'Don't be a bad girl! Don't be bad! Eat your sprouts *now*!'

I could see a tantrum coming on and decided to nip it in the bud. I put a hand on his shoulder. 'Trevor, it's fine – if Juliet doesn't want to eat her sprouts, that's all right. We don't make anyone here eat what they don't want.'

He was nearly choking with anxiety now. But when he saw that I wasn't angry and that the sprouts were cleaned off the plate without any repercussions for anyone, he eventually calmed down. It took a while, though. This was clearly associated with some real trauma and made me wonder where it had come from.

The social worker had told me about a woman who worked at the residential home, a woman named Keira, who had developed a bit of a friendship with the boy. It was as much of a friendship as he seemed to have had. I decided that Keira and I needed to talk.

The next day, after I'd taken him to school, I popped in and found Keira and had a chat.

She was a hardworking woman who had been at the home for several years. She was glad to have the job there, and loved the children, but she let me know that she was not entirely happy with the way the nuns did things. 'I'm afraid they were quite hard on Trevor.'

'Were they?' I tried not to get angry. 'How do you mean?'

'Well, they expect the children to be obedient at all times – and you know how Trevor can be.'

'I suppose his tantrums were not welcome.'

'And his toilet accidents. They have no patience at all for that in a boy his age.'

She glanced around. Dear God, she was as frightened of the nuns as any of the children. In a low voice, she said, 'I tried to help him out, help him clean things up so that the nuns didn't find out.'

'Well, thank you for that.'

She shook her head. 'Ah, it didn't always help. If it wasn't one thing, it was another.'

'Like what?'

'They're also very strict about eating everything on your plate at lunchtime. They have problems with some of the children about that – especially when they have sprouts.' She glanced around again. 'A lot of kids don't like sprouts. I don't like 'em much myself. But no one is allowed to leave them on their plate.'

'What happens if they do?'

Keira looked very unhappy. 'They're dragged off to Sister Vianney's office and get punished.'

'Caned, I suppose?'

She nodded. 'Yes, usually on the legs. Which I think is particularly cruel, considering.'

'Considering what?'

'Well, they really do get dragged to her office some-times. I've seen it. There's a carpet runs down the hall, and

I've seen little Trevor dragged down that carpet in his shorts. I know it must have scraped his legs something dreadful.'

I knew that nuns still believed in physical punishment for kids, smacking, caning and so forth. I thought it was crude, barbaric and unnecessary, but I knew it happened. But the extent of the abuse they were inflicting – emotional, physical, psychological: what kind of people did this to a six-year-old boy?

'Bloody hell, Keira! Have you said anything to anyone?'

She blanched. 'I told his foster parents a little bit about what was going on when he moved out. But look here.' She glanced around again, really worried now. 'I do what I can to help, but I can't lose my job.'

I nodded. She was stuck, all right. She wanted to do something, but she had children of her own to feed and was truly terrified that she would be out of work if she blew the whistle. I wouldn't say I sympathized but I understood.

I went home with a lot on my mind. I needed to put a stop to this, but I wasn't sure how to proceed. It seemed there were two problems here. I needed to undo, as much as I could, the damage that had been done to Trevor, and stop it continuing with the other children living in that wretched place.

In the meantime, it was getting close to Christmas and we included Trevor in all of our preparations for the holidays. One night, we put up the tree and I got out the boxes of lights, decorations and tinsel so the kids could do the decorating.

I opened one of the boxes that was full of loads of ornaments. Sharon reached in, picked one up – and all hell broke loose. Trevor went ballistic. 'No, no! Don't touch it! Don't touch it! Put it down, put it down, put it down!' He had gone from normality into full-blown, incandescent, mindless terror in less than a second.

Sharon just stood there with the bauble in her hand, staring at him as if he was the world's biggest gobshite. I knew this would not work out well.

'I can pick it up if I want to. See?' She kept it dangling from her hand. 'And, look, I'm picking up another one! Lookit – I can pick up as many as I want!'

I was afraid Trevor's eyes would pop out of his head. I couldn't help but notice that he wasn't having an angry tantrum: he was genuinely afraid for Sharon, afraid that something terrible would happen to her. One of the twins decided to get in on the fun and picked up an ornament as well.

This was more than Trevor could take. He swung his arm, trying to knock them out of the girls' hands. 'No, no, no!' he was screaming. 'If you touch those, the devil will burn your fingers! He'll burn your fingers right off!'

Well, that shut up everyone in the room.

Sharon and little Katie just froze, not sure what to do or think.

I walked over to Trevor, picked up a red glassy orna-ment from the box and handed it to him. He just stared, tears running down his face. 'Trevor, maybe someone told you that if you touch the Christmas decorations you'll be punished.' And I could just imagine who that was. Sister

Vianney had moved up to Public Enemy Number One on my list. 'But here at our house, it's perfectly all right to touch them. And guess what?'

He looked up at me, not sure what might be coming next.

'Even if one gets broken, it's completely all right.'

The rest of that evening turned into a therapy session more than an evening of tree-decorating. Slowly, bit by bit, we got to the point where Trevor wasn't afraid to let one of the other children touch the decorations and had proved to him that he could touch them himself and not get his fingers burned off by the devil. It may sound like a silly notion, but he was petrified. Someone had hammered this into him – and hammered hard.

It was a revelation for him when he found out that it was safe to touch the decorations in our house. I began to wonder what other frightening nonsense those nuns had been putting into his head.

After the Christmas break, I informed Social Services that Trevor could stay with us for as long as he needed to. Which I guessed would probably be for ever. And I came up with another plan as well.

I knew that he was still carrying around a lot of baggage from his previous experience at the residential home. I had been dealing with troubled children for a good while and had learned a lot about the concept of 'closure'. I decided that some closure would do Trevor good.

We went back to his old home for a brief visit. I set up an appointment for him to talk to the head of the place, the infamous Sister Vianney. As we sat outside the gates, in my car, Trevor started to have second thoughts. Just the sight of the front door was giving him a panic attack.

I put my hand on his shoulder. 'It's all right, Trevor – you just say exactly what we talked about and don't worry a fig about anything she says to you. I'll be right here, so you come back out of that door when you've finished.'

He nodded and walked off.

And this was what happened.

He went through the door and into Sister Vianney's office. She stood up and came around her desk. She was a tall, severe woman, with heavy creases on each side of her mouth that were seemingly never elevated by a smile.

'Well, Trevor, it's you, is it?'

He started to lose his nerve.

'Yes, Sister,' he managed to squeak.

'You're with yet another foster family, are you?'

'Yes, Sister.'

'Hmm. You seem to be a very naughty boy wherever you go. I've heard a bit about this new foster mother of yours, this Rio woman.' She leaned over. 'And she probably doesn't like you any more than any of the others did.'

At that something in Trevor snapped. Or perhaps it was just that something finally healed and came together. But at any rate he blurted, 'Well, Rio says I can stay with her as long as I want and I like it there and I think you can just *fuck off*!' With that he turned and ran out of the door.

It's a good thing he ran because she came tearing along behind him, yelling at the top of her voice.

As Trevor flew out of the front door, I saw the beastly

vision of the tall, dreadful woman in her plain jumper and sensible shoes directly behind him. He hopped into the front seat and locked his door. She came to my side of the car and banged on my window.

Most of what she was blathering was unintelligible, but when I rolled the window down a bit, I could hear her yapping about how she would report this, and how despicable his behaviour was, and how she would make sure I never got to foster another child.

I gave her a good long look and said, 'You're the one who has no business having anything to do with children and I am going to raise holy hell until I see this place closed down.'

Her mouth snapped shut. 'You're being ridiculous.'

I put the car into gear, and shouted, 'We'll see!' as I drove off. In the rear-view mirror, I could see her yelling and gesticulating at the car, nearly foaming at the mouth with frustration.

Trevor turned to look too, then turned back to me. And we both giggled.

I started a campaign about that residential home that went to everyone I could think of. I would have taken it to the Pope if I'd had to. After Trevor came into my full-time care, I had a house that was filled to bursting. As a foster parent, I was entitled to some assistance so I asked Social Services for a home helper for us. That made a huge difference, let me tell you. I then started to get together documentation of the systematic abuse that had been going on at the residential home for years. Trevor was one of many, many children who had been emotionally scarred by the nuns' horrific behaviour.

As word got out about what I was doing, other people came forward to tell me what they knew. It was an ugly picture indeed.

It took nearly two years, but that home was closed, never to reopen.

Sister Vianney took early retirement. Very early. And she was never allowed to work with children again.

And if you're wondering whether I was upset with Trevor for what he'd said to the sister that day, don't even go there. That was what I had told him to say. I may not be a therapist, but I think I know a thing or two about closure.

17

My life was not all work and raising kids. Summer holidays were one of the highlights of the year. This tradition had started back when we were all young and single, and the addition of spouses and infants didn't change it. They weren't just family affairs but tended to include a random assortment of friends and relations that more closely resembled a travelling circus.

So it was that one particular summer there were seven adults, five children, three musical instruments, and two vans of us on the road, with Doris, Hughie and myself taking turns to drive. Our plan was to have no plan and that always seemed to work out for the best. We took off on a Friday afternoon and headed west, towards the sea. We got to County Clare and kept heading west. We eventually landed in a fairy-tale place called Doolin.

At night we always managed to find a pub where we could join in with the music, and during the day we had loads of things to do. Gorgeous scenery to walk through, sheep that the children were sure wanted to be chased, and we could go to the shore and let the kids splash around. And there on the horizon, floating like pieces of a broken dream, were the Aran Islands: Inishmore, Inishmaan and Inisheer. As soon as I saw them, I knew I wanted to go.

The easy way, of course, would have been to take the ferry. That would also be the most expensive way. Fortunately I had connections.

One evening a big fella with a personality too large to be contained in such a small pub had rolled into the session. He knew everyone there and had been telling them some uproarious stories in Irish. When he noticed the load of us interlopers, he deigned to grace us with his stories in English. It wasn't too long before we were told that we were in the presence of Rory, the self-proclaimed King of Inisheer.

According to him, his was a small but mighty kingdom, mostly 'peopled' by sheep and donkeys. And lonely, apparently: he was the only one who recognized his divine right to rule. He made his living as a farmer and fisherman and I was immediately drawn to his larger-than-life personality and his infectious humour. Even more importantly, he told us he had a nice currach.

Being city folk, we didn't know what that might mean — indeed, the way he said it we thought it sounded kind of suggestive — but it turned out that a currach was a type of boat. It's the traditional Irish boat of the islands, small and canoe-like, made of hides stretched over a wooden frame. Well, I don't think Rory was that staunch a traditionalist. No one really used hides any more. A waterproof canvas was more the norm. But it was still a very different thing from the usual boat — no solid planking under your feet, for a start. It seemed Rory would sail or paddle (depending on the weather) his currach from the island to Doolin and back, and I thought that sounded marvellous.

I convinced him to take myself and Doris over one afternoon.

The weather was dry, but the sky was frowning with puckered clouds that were biding their time until it would be most inconvenient for the rainfall. The sea was, according to Rory, only mildly choppy. Good God. I was trying to imagine what very choppy was like.

We had to take our shoes off, wade into the water a bit, then climb into the currach. The breeze was strong, but not gusty, and Rory had the sail up. He shoved us away from the shore and we headed to the island.

Rory nattered the whole time, full of stories of fish and whales and seabirds and shipwrecks. It made the time fly. At one point, a particularly aggressive wave knocked us a bit sideways and Doris and I lurched dangerously close to the edge of the boat.

'Watch out there! Hold on tight!' the King commanded.

'No worries,' I said. 'I can swim.'

Rory snorted. 'Bloody useless, that.'

'Swimming? I would think it's about the best thing someone in a currach could know.'

He snorted again. Regally, I'm sure. 'No man who travels in a currach would waste his time learning to swim.'

I thought he was being deliberately difficult. But if he was trying to bait me to ask, I was willing to oblige. 'Really? And why ever not?' I refrained from adding 'you big lummox'.

'Because,' he leaned towards us as if imparting the wisdom of the ages, 'if a sea is rough enough to capsize one of these beauties,' he smacked the edge of the boat, 'then it's a sea what can't be swum in anyways. So it's best not to struggle and just drown quick, like.'

I gulped. And held on to the currach very tightly the rest of the trip.

The beach we landed on was rocky and grey. It was a glorious afternoon. We walked all over the island, met many other farmers and fishing folk and had some views of the sea that made me literally gasp with delight. We made our way to Rory's farm, which was also mainly rock, snuggled up to his kitchen fire and told each other stories while we clutched mugs of piping hot tea. It was truly lovely.

But His Majesty was saving a particular treat for us. 'Honoured guests,' he announced, 'it is time for a drink.'

Doris and I were expecting a sherry, or perhaps a nice sip of whiskey. Even a brandy, if he was being particularly extravagant. But the King had different plans. He went over to a cupboard and took out some small glasses. There was a solemnity to his movements that made me think we were in for something. Then he came back to the table with a bottle that bore no label, containing a clear liquid.

Oh dear.

'Now, girls,' he said, pulling the cork out of the top of the bottle, 'you can't leave my island without a taste of the mother's milk.'

As soon as the liquid hit the glass, my eyes started to burn from the vapours. Doris looked as if she had just been asked to swallow a frog.

'Is that what I think it is?' I asked.

'It is, if you think it's God's gift to the Irish.' He filled three small glasses, then lifted his and held it to the light. 'My own homemade *poitín*!'

And as a general rule, *poitín* is considered more suitable for cleaning carburettors than for human consumption. I was no teetotaller but *poitín* was something I had managed to avoid my entire life. The stories I had heard about it were daunting, to say the least.

Rory held out his glass and seemed to be waiting for us to do the same. I glanced sideways at Doris and managed to give her an encouraging nod. We lifted our glasses, clinked them with Rory's to a cry of '*Sláinte!*' then watched as he neatly knocked his back in a single swallow. When his head didn't disintegrate into flames, I decided to follow his example, as a polite guest should. I scrunched my eyes shut, tilted my wrist and swallowed it in a blink.

A white-hot poker of meat-devouring heat skewered itself down my throat and into my solar plexus, like a lightning strike. Something red and flaming exploded behind my eyes. I think it was my brain.

I heard a whimper and knew that Doris had downed hers as well. As I managed to take a breath and open my eyes I saw her, head back, hands pounding the table top. I tried to speak. I think nothing but small blue flames erupted from my lips. Rory looked at us and smiled hugely. Doris was still pounding the table. I was trying to get my eyes back into focus.

'Not bad for your first go, girls,' he continued, and refilled the glasses. 'That was a good warm-up.'

I tried to say, 'Warm-up?' but instead I made a sound

that was more like a sheep trying to bleat in a way that would be meaningful to a baleen whale.

Rory continued to smile, the twinkle in his eyes looking more and more to me as if it had been kindled by the flames from Satan's own soul. Oh, wait a minute, no, that was just a lighted match in his hand.

'Now,' he said, 'time to learn to drink it properly.' He waved the match over the surface of his glass and silvery flames appeared.

He raised it, gave us a big smile and a wink, said something fairly long, yet I'm sure very meaningful, in Irish, then knocked it back.

The first glass of *poitín* was already doing a number on me.

'Did you just drink that?' I burbled.

Doris added, 'It was on flame ... lighted ... It was burning.' She threw up her hands.

He waved another lighted match over our drinks. 'It's the best way to have it.' He pushed our glasses back at us. 'But there's a trick to it.'

My immediate thought: Not having a brain? That would be the best strategy.

He leaned forward. 'Never, ever drink it while it's really on fire.' He put one finger up alongside his nose. 'Just before you gulp it down, you blow it out – like this.'

He picked up my glass and, in what seemed to be slow motion, he lifted it to his lips, took a deep breath, exhaled across the top of the glass, then gulped it down.

'Thash brilliant,' I said.

He refilled my glass and also rekindled it. 'All right now, lassies,' he said, pouring more for himself. '*Sláinte!*'

I don't remember much of the rest of the day. But the next morning Doris and I got into the currach to head back to Doolin. Doris had a head on her the size of one of the neighbouring islands. I had to wrap her in a blanket and get her comfortable. I felt surprisingly good. Not exactly clear-headed, mind you, but pretty fit, considering.

Rory claimed I had a good head on me for drink. No doubt I have an excellent liver also. At any rate, we got back to Doolin and had one last night there of music, then had to pack everyone up and get us all back to Dublin. We hated to go, but from then on, whenever we could get away for a day or two, we'd make a beeline for Doolin. Sometimes I believe in Providence: it was surely a Providential gift to stumble on that magical place.

As it turned out, my drinking lesson did me a good turn later. Besides dancing, Doris and I were very involved in the Dublin music scene, joining in with the likes of Luke Kelly and Ronnie Drew. We had become known as singers and were established as regulars at many of the music venues around the city. Now Sean, one of our musical acquaintances, had organized a trip for Doris, a few others and me to go and sing, dance and do all our usual tomfoolery in an Irish bar in New York. I had never set foot in America before and New York City was dazzling. I considered myself to be a city girl and I thought, Well, New York is just another big city, right? But the sheer size and energy of it knocked me off my feet. There's a constant hum in the place, a throbbing of humanity and commerce that pervades everything. It's such a vital, invigorating atmosphere, so different from the leisurely pace at home. But what can I say? Everywhere you go people seem to love the Irish, and especially in New York. Everyone made us feel welcome and at home. We settled in, organized our evening entertainment of songs, stories and dancing, and had them packed in every night.

Besides some singing, one of my main jobs was storytelling. I would tell stories about the leprechauns, the faerie folk, Tir na nÓg and what-not. I would start with something that I remembered my granddad telling me – but then my imagination would always take wing and I would unravel some completely new tale that just seemed like a good one at the time. Quite often I would start with some idea – 'There was once a dragonfly that wanted to be a real dragon' – and just keep going, not really knowing where it would end. It always went down a treat, but after a few weeks, we started getting repeat customers and they would ask me to retell a story they had heard before. And there I was, unable to remember a word of it. Once the story was told, it was out of my head. But when they asked, I would start again and try to tell a story that had some semblance to what I had made up the time before. No doubt I quite often left them baffled, wondering why the 'genuine' Irish folktale had mutated into something different.

It wasn't all work. We had some evenings off and we used them to enjoy the New York night life. One evening in particular, we ended up in – of all places – yet another Irish bar. Wouldn't you think we'd had enough of Irish bars? But I guess we just couldn't resist the idea of being the *real* Irish people in the place. Doris and a couple of the others had figured out that being Irish was generally good enough to get us a free drink.

The place we went to that night was no exception. As soon as they heard our accents, the big blokes drinking at the bar (who claimed to be Irish American) bought us all drinks and wanted to chat about the 'old country'. As usually happened, we got onto the legendary capacity that the Irish are supposed to have for drinking. A couple of the fellas in our group did the customary – and expected – bragging as to how much they could imbibe. The Americans accepted it good-naturedly.

But then one big fella, named Ray, decided that the Irishmen's claim to bragging rights was not satisfactory. 'Hey, Bill!' he called to the barman. 'Bring out the bottle of the good stuff!'

There was a hush in the bar. Everyone but us seemed to know what that meant.

The barman appeared with a dingy bottle of clear liquid. Oh, no.

'Now, we separate the men from the boys!' Ray lifted the bottle. 'We got us some real po-cheen here. And I'm betting,' he looked around at the Irish lads, 'that none of you can outdrink me with this!'

Ray was about six feet four and weighed close to three hundred pounds. Judging by the looks on the lads' faces, they did not disagree with him.

'Aw, come on!' Ray reached into his pocket, pulled out his wallet and slapped five twenty-dollar bills on the bar. 'I got a hundred dollars says I can outlast you bog-trotters at your own drink.'

The lads were eyeing the cash, but still not stepping up to the task. They were Irish, after all – they *knew* what drinking *poitín* could do. The next thing *I* knew, there were hands shoved in my back and Doris was pushing me forward. 'She'll take the bet!'

Ray and the lads watched as Doris pushed and pulled me to the front. Ray was amused at first. Then, when the other American fellas started to snicker, he looked very annoyed. It was not a pleasant sight to see Ray annoyed.

I whispered to Doris, 'What in the name of Hell are you doing?'

'Rio, you can do this.'

Now I was facing Ray. He towered over me. I think if he could have squashed me with his boot heel, he would have.

'You?' he snarled.

Well, I didn't need that kind of attitude from a meat-head such as himself. He had called us bog-trotters. That could not go unanswered. 'That's right,' I said, and gave him my biggest grin. 'Don't worry.' I nudged him with my elbow. 'I'll go easy on ya.'

More snickering. I heard the lads behind me saying something, but Doris told them to shut up and that she knew what she was doing. Well, I was glad *she* knew what she was doing.

There was no graceful way for Ray to back out now. The barman brought us two small glasses and filled them with the clear liquid that looked as if it would very likely dissolve a human skull.

I reached for my glass.

'Oh, no.' Ray pulled it away. 'Not yet.'

He produced a lighter and set the surface of his drink on fire. All of his companions and most of the rest of the bar gasped, then hooted and roared.

'My hundred dollars,' he announced, 'says this little gal here can't drink it like this.'

He raised the glass, gave me a shit-eating grin and downed it. His face turned a bit purple, but he raised the glass again and the bar erupted with shouts and claps.

He eyeballed me, then flicked his lighter and set the top of my drink on fire.

'That's part of the rules,' he said. 'The po-cheen has to be drunk the real Irish way.'

He turned to his friends. 'It's all over now, boys.'

Someone behind me said, 'Rio, you don't have to do this,' but Doris shushed him.

I kept my eyes on Ray and never blinked. I picked up my glass, drew a deep breath, ever so quickly blew the flame out, then knocked it back – and slapped the empty glass on the bar with a crack.

I grinned at him again. His friends were stunned, then started laughing and slapping him on the back.

'You're in for it now, big guy,' they were saying. I reached for the one hundred dollars.

Ray's hand snapped out. 'Oh no you don't. I got another hundred bucks says you can't do that again.'

Now the rest of my Irish gang was behind me. Especially now they had seen that I had not burst into flames, fainted or started babbling like a drunken idiot. Yet.

'Come on, Rio – sure you can do it!'

The entire bar seemed to have turned into a stadium and Ray and I were the match of the day. So be it. Game on.

The Americans would slap money on the bar, the barman would pour, Ray would light the drinks, then we'd knock them back to a tumult of shouts and cheers. At some point someone asked me if I wanted to sit down. I knew that would be a mistake. No, it was to the last man (or person) standing. If I didn't remain on my feet, I knew I would never be able to get back on them.

Ray, no doubt, thought he would have me after two. Maybe three. But we got to five and he had beads of sweat on his forehead.

We got to six and his hand was starting to wobble when he ignited the *poitín*.

By eight, he had to get one of his friends to do it.

Finally, there was nine hundred dollars on the bar. It seemed appropriate, as I felt like I had about nine hundred living brain cells left in my head. At the most.

Keeping my eyes locked on Ray's sweaty brow, I knocked back number nine. Our glasses cracked on the table. I tried to give him my usual smile – it felt a bit lopsided and I think I was drooling a little.

As everyone cheered and someone started chanting, 'Number ten! Number ten!' it seemed as if the world was melting a little bit. No, it was Ray.

One minute he was standing there, empty glass in his hand – he was still gripping it after slamming it onto the bar. Then he was sliding to the floor in a slow-moving avalanche, like an ice-cream cone next to a sunbed. There was a thud, and there he was – in a heap, at the feet of his loyal supporters.

A huge yell went up, mostly from my Irish group. There were lots of cheers and shouts and back-slapping. Doris was smart enough to realize they had better not slap *me* on the back. No telling what that would bring up. She came to me and started to scoop up the money.

'Hold up!' It was Ray's mate, and he seemed to be taking charge now that his huge friend was basically a puddle. 'You have to be able to walk out the door on your own two feet. Then the money is yours.' His friends agreed, noisily.

I looked at Doris. 'Give the money to one of our lads. You go outside and wait for me by the door.'

'You sure?'

I nodded. My head felt wobbly. Doris had three eyes in the middle of her forehead and her mouth was upside-down. I made a mental note to discuss that with her later.

She headed out of the door.

I turned to the American lads. 'Right! I'm off now. Thanksh for the drink.' I tried to give what I thought was a jaunty wave. I stepped away from the bar carefully, not wanting to tread on Ray. He was curled up on his friend's feet. I wasn't sure, but it looked like he was also sucking his thumb.

'Before you go . . .' His friend put a hand on my arm. 'Where did you learn to drink like that?'

I grinned and put one finger on the side of my nose. 'From the King!' I announced.

Still grinning, I turned and made for the door. It seemed to be about a mile and a half, but I knew I had to get to it, open it, then walk outside or all that lovely money would go right back into those American pockets. Lift one foot, now the other, I kept telling myself. My God, the door didn't seem to be any closer.

As I passed one of the onlookers sitting at a table, he turned to his friend and I heard him say, 'She learned how to drink flaming po-cheen from Elvis?'

I couldn't take the time to explain to him about Rory, the King of Inisheer, who, by now, like Elvis, had passed to the great beyond. I just kept putting one foot in front of the other. Then the door handle. Then I was outside.

I heard an eruption of screams and shouts – and groans – from inside the bar and knew that it was over. I had made it.

Doris came up, took me by the elbow and – BOOM. My knees buckled and I went straight to the pavement.

I don't remember anything that happened immediately after, but I'm told that the lads came out, I was carried to the flat where we were staying and they tucked me in. And, I am happy to say, we all got to tuck some American money into our pockets.

As they say, the show must go on. As soon as I was on my feet again, it was back to business as usual at our New York show.

One evening a fella came into the bar to see it – and it was obvious that he was not your ordinary punter. He was accompanied by two huge brutes who shadowed him constantly. The man himself was a smallish fella, with thinning hair, but wearing an impressively expensive suit. One of the big brutes sat at the table with him, but never ate or drank, just constantly scanned the room. The other took up a strategic position near a back wall, where he could eyeball everyone who came in.

I saw other folks at nearby tables looking at yer man and whispering. But no one dared approach him. The brute at the table with him had a bulge under his jacket that I did not think meant he was happy to see anybody.

We did our show as usual, and our important guest enjoyed it immensely, hooting and clapping and joining in with some of the songs. He was a fine singer himself.

At the end, he came up to us (one of the brutes at his shoulder was looking at us the same way that exterminators look at beetles just before they set off bug bombs) and went on and on about how much he had enjoyed it. He asked if we had had dinner yet.

Sean said no, and that was it: our exalted guest insisted on buying full dinners for all of us. Some tables were pushed together and he sat down with us, while we scraped our plates and sloshed our beer. Although he wasn't an Irishman, he loved the music and the lore, and was an absolute expert in how to have a good time. More songs were sung as we sat around the table, and many, many jokes were told as the two brutes stood like statues, looking as sour as when they had first come in.

Finally, the dinner ended and in the wee hours it was time for our genial guest to take his brutes and go. Before he slipped away, I managed to get close enough to him to say a word or two: 'It was very kind of you to give us dinner,' I told him, before one of the brutes could mistake me for an assassin.

He turned back to me, blue eyes twinkling, and said, 'Hey, babe, not at all. Had a great time – thanks to all of you for a really great evening.'

'No, no,' I said. 'Thank *you*, Mr Sinatra.'

He winked, and then his brutes whisked him away.

18

I imagine that people who knew us thought of Doris and myself as a team. It was rare to find one of us without the other, and there weren't too many aspects of our lives that we didn't share. The girls who had swanned around the dance halls of Dublin, who had travelled across the ocean to sing and tell stories together, had become the hard-edged women who worked together, despaired over our children, and still carried their humour and dreams together. We weren't inseparable – one of the reasons we were able to stay so close was that we were also able to give each other space. But, ultimately, there was no one in my life whom I counted on more, whom I depended on more, or who made me laugh anywhere near as much.

And then, after more than thirty years of this tandem existence, I found myself blindingly, homicidally, furious with her. I would have killed her – if she hadn't already been dying.

I know my anger was misdirected. But I was completely, unrestrainedly angry – with her, God, everything and everyone because it seemed they were all letting me down.

Doris had cancer. She had known for months and hadn't told me. And she had been given only months to live.

She had wanted to spare me, I suppose, so she had

spent those months when she knew what was ahead of her dealing with it alone. Maybe that was what hurt the worst – that after everything we had shared, after being up to our noses in each other's business for so long, after she had been the only shoulder I had ever leaned on, we had not shared this.

At the very end, she was in the hospital. By that time, all they could do was try and keep her pain bearable, though it was constant. I went to visit her as often as I could – there was very little of her left to visit. She had been whittled down to a twig, and the morphine kept her in a cloud of fuzzy memories and imagined landscapes. Sometimes she knew me. Most of the time she knew only the crazy meanderings that were going on in her head. I would sit by her all the same, no matter what she rambled and raved or mumbled about.

In those small spaces when she was quiet, I would talk to her about the old times. Retell stories of things we had done to remind her that she'd been a crazy, mad thing even back when she was well. She would have liked to remember that.

I tried, even then, to imagine what my life would be like without her. I couldn't. It was like trying to imagine there was no sky. It was very much like knowing there was no ground beneath my feet.

The day she died, I wasn't there. I had gone to attend some big family do – it had seemed important at the time. When I discovered she had passed over without me there to say goodbye, I didn't know what to do with myself. In all of my years, I had come across many grief-stricken people. I had always commiserated with them over their loss – how could you not? But until the moment I lost Doris, I had not really known what that kind of grief felt like. I had not known that there could be such an obliterating emptiness where my heart had been.

For Doris, at the end of her ordeal, they had been able to ease the pain that tormented her. But what was there for me? How was I supposed to make mine bearable?

The first few days I operated like a mechanical device – every day had its prescribed tasks that needed to be accomplished, and that meant I didn't have to think about what to do, I could just do it. I had several children with me at the time – Lily, Trevor, the twins and Sharon. Doris's own twin boys were grown-up and had been living away for a while. They dealt with their grief with the resilience of youth. My own strength seemed to have deserted me: it had drained away day by day as I had sat next to her in that sterile hospital room. Now I had nothing left. And in spite of the people who depended on me and needed me, I felt as if I had no one, no one who would understand how lost I felt. Doris had been the only friend who had ever been there when I was hanging at the end of my tether. In a house full of people, and a life that ran me ragged with places to go and things to do, I had never felt so alone.

The bustle of the daily run-around kept me functioning while the kids needed me. But at night the pain would set in, full-blown and hungry. I would lie down and close my eyes and the tears would start without any let-up. Instead of sleep and dreams, I spent hours racked with sobbing and would get up in the morning puffy-eyed and irritable, nearly insane with grief and guilt.

At first, the kids tiptoed around me, knowing that I was keeping up a fragile façade. But, of course, they healed faster than I ever could, and the forward momentum of their lives carried them through. They would not have understood that I was still stuck in my own private mire of heartbreak. For their sakes, I managed to act as if I had also moved on. But it got harder and harder as the days went by and I was still unable to rest. I became forgetful and my temper was so brittle that no one knew what would send me into a tirade. Something big, like a broken window, I would shrug off. A shoe at the bottom of the stairs might provoke me into an incandescent fury.

I knew I was losing it.

19

It won't make much sense for me to tell you how much I unravelled unless you understand that I was not normally the unravelling type.

A case in point. One Sunday morning, in the years when we were ace street traders, Doris and I had arrived at the market very early as usual. Our van was stuffed with a load of goods we knew would have a quick turnaround. Packs of toilet paper and kitchen rolls, cans of mushy peas that were only slightly dented, assorted dishes and cookware.

As we were unloading, I spotted Nan and Tess across the way. Nan was standing behind a table that had a flowery plastic covering, but was otherwise nearly empty. She was trying to arrange a couple of cracked ceramic teapots and a stack of plastic cups so that it would look as if the table were full. Behind her I could see the lank yellow hair of her son Robert, his head just barely above the back of his wheelchair. Tess was pouring herself a cup of tea from a flask, her hands shaking. She was struggling with diabetes, I knew, and often had bouts where she was tired. But every Sunday she and Nan were there. The extra money was a life-saver for them – but on that morning things were looking a bit bleak.

I wandered over and said hello.

Nan gave me a weary smile, Tess handed me the cup of tea in her hand. 'Here you go,' she said. 'Warm ya up a bit.'

I handed it right back to her. 'Not at all, I'm warm enough. Let me help you unpack the rest of your things. Hey there, Robert. How are you on this Sunday morning?'

He smiled and shrugged a shoulder – I knew it was his way of waving hello. The muscular dystrophy had left him without much use of his arms, but he was always cheerful.

Tess set the cup down. 'No worries, we're all unpacked.'

I looked at the table. Pathetic didn't even begin to describe it.

When I looked back at Tess she knew exactly what I was thinking. 'The van broke down this week so we weren't able to collect much,' she said.

'Could you not even get to Leyden's?'

Leyden's was a wholesaler on Dublin's northside. They sometimes offered good deals on bulk items – you weren't going to make as good a profit as if you'd got it yourself direct, but they always had some things you could turn around quickly.

Tess shook her head.

'Well, there's my van and we've emptied it. Let's pop over to Leyden's now and get you sorted.'

Tess grabbed a handbag from behind the table. 'That'd be brilliant, Rio, thanks.'

Nan grabbed my hand. 'You're very good. Thanks a million.'

'No problem. Come on, Tess. Let's get over there before all the good ones are gone.'

When we arrived, Leyden's was already busy. Lots of

traders were there making last-minute buys. I liked to think that I was usually one of the more savvy ones because I got all of my wholesale buying done during the week. But Tess had not had that luxury. While she was examining boxes of cleaning-liquid bottles with slightly squashed lids, I was poking around to see what else – and who else – was around.

I noticed that a few folks were buzzing around the stacks of toilet rolls – and I also noticed that Leyden's wholesale price was five pence higher than I had paid. I felt rather smug.

The feeling was shattered by a clatter of feet and shouting that seemed to roll across the crowd of us like a wave.

I turned just as three men with black balaclavas pulled over their faces shoved their way to the cash registers and jumped on the counters, yelling something about a robbery.

It seemed so ridiculous that at first I thought it was a joke.

When one of the men waved a shotgun, I knew I was wrong.

The air split with the sound of screaming, and for a moment I feared being crushed by the panicked mob more than being shot by an idiot with a gun that looked too big for him.

'EVERYBODY DOWN!' the gun-carrying fella screamed, waving the black barrels in a way that was meant to be menacing.

I fell to the floor in a heap with everyone else. I lifted

my head just a bit to try to locate Tess, but couldn't see a sign of her.

While the one fella kept waving his gun, the other two hopped down and forced the cashiers to empty their registers into some grubby sacks. None of us knew at that moment that one of the cashiers had managed to push the button that was a silent alarm. While the masked men rushed from register to register, filling bag after bag, the police were already on their way. And the nearest garda station wasn't far away.

They hadn't finished filling the last sacks when we heard the sound of the sirens.

Now it was the fellas in the masks who were in a panic.

'Shit! Shit! Shit!' the fella with the gun was screaming.

The sound of the police cars had made everyone on the floor lift their heads and start looking around. This sent the man with the gun into a panic.

'EVERYONE STAY DOWN!' His voice was shrill now and didn't seem anywhere near as intimidating as that of a man with a double-barrelled shotgun should.

As the police pounded on the doors, the rest of us thought maybe it was time to scramble. The man with the shotgun disagreed.

'I SAID TO STAY BLOODY DOWN!' He was frantic.

When everyone just looked at him, he punctuated his orders by pointing the shotgun at the ceiling and squeezing the trigger. The blast was huge, and if anyone had had any doubts as to whether he was willing to use his weapon, those doubts were erased. The terror he had meant to instil in us, though, was tempered by the plaster and pow-der from the ceiling that proceeded to fall on his head. He had to waggle it to shake the dust out of his eyes and took a moment to wipe it away from his nose just before he sneezed.

Much as I wanted to, I didn't giggle. Like everyone else, I went back to lying face down on the floor.

The banging on the doors had become more intense and the robbers gathered together to decide what to do. After a heated exchange, the one with the gun turned and started pointing to people on the floor.

'That one,' he would signal with the barrels of his gun, 'and that one.' And the other two would go over and grab the person he had pointed to. They were gathering them all together, standing them in a little group, and I thought, Are they going to shoot them? What are they doing?

A phone rang at one of the registers. The girl next to it just stared at it, afraid to move. The man with the shotgun waved both barrels at her. 'Answer it!'

She jumped and snatched the receiver. With eyes as big as billiard balls, she whispered, 'Hello?'

After a moment she just nodded and held the phone out. 'It's the police. They want to talk to you.'

One of the fellas without a gun walked over and grabbed it. He turned his back to us and we heard a lot of agitated talk, but I couldn't make out exactly what he was saying. Finally he yelled something obscene and slammed the phone down. After a few minutes of conversation with his companions, he turned to the crowd of us lying on the floor.

'Listen up!' he shouted. 'We've just told the guards that if they don't let us outta here with the money, we're going to start shooting hostages.'

The people they had gathered together gasped. One man's knees buckled and the woman next to him caught him awkwardly by the elbow. I could hear someone sobbing.

The man with the shotgun spoke up: 'We'll need a few more than that.'

'All right.' The first fella reached down, yanked a young man from the floor and shoved him towards the group. Then he reached down for another – and grabbed Tess.

As he shoved her towards the other hostages I could see her shaking, her lips trembling as she tried not to cry.

I jumped up.

Not a good idea, really. Slow movements would have gone down much better with that lot.

Shotgun man went bananas. 'I SAID TO STAY DOWN!'

I couldn't see under his balaclava, but I suspect he was foaming at the mouth. I raised my hands, like I'd seen them do in the cowboy movies. 'Please, take me and not her. She's sick.'

He paused. The other two men were busy trying to herd all of the hostages to the other side of the room but they turned to look. 'Wha'?'

'The one there that you just took. She's not well.'

Fortunately Tess was shaking even more when she realized they were all looking at her and that helped prove my point.

The first fella walked towards me. 'How do you know she's sick?'

'She's my friend. She has diabetes.'

Behind his balaclava I saw him blink. Apparently he didn't know what diabetes was or perhaps it didn't sound serious enough. I tried again. 'And she's appo-eppo-appocoleptic.'

I wasn't sure what it was, and Tess had no such thing, but it had what I thought was a very serious ring to it.

He blinked again, but licked his lips in a way that made me think I'd worried him a bit.

The third fella, who had been pretty quiet so far, finally spoke up: 'Jesus, we don't need someone havin' fits or some such. Take yer one there. She looks healthy enough.'

So, with an impolite shove, they propelled Tess back towards the group on the floor and the man with the mask grabbed my arm.

I had gone into the store as a disinterested customer. Now I was a life-at-stake hostage.

They managed to herd us through a back door into a storeroom. Two of them eventually smuggled us out into an alleyway and into an old rust bucket of a van. I was crammed into the dirty, smelly thing, with all of the doors and windows closed, with five other panic-stricken people. The two robbers who stayed with us included the one with the shotgun. The third remained inside the building where he stayed on the phone, talking to the police. Some sort of negotiations were going on, but we never knew what they were.

I looked at the faces of the people with me in the van.

One woman was crying silently, but continuously. A man was pale green in the face. After about ten minutes he broke into a sweat.

The one with the shotgun was sitting in the front seat, facing his companion, who was behind the wheel, but with the gun angled towards us.

I said to him, 'Yer man here is going to get sick.'

He jerked his head around. 'Wha'?' The end of the shotgun poked disconcertingly in my direction.

'He's green at the gills. He's going to be sick.'

The greenish man moaned in what I took to be agreement.

The one behind the wheel turned. 'Ah, fuck. You need to get him outta here. I'm not gonna clean that up.'

The shotgun man snapped back at him: 'I'm holding a fucking shotgun! You get him out.'

Clearly unhappy, the driver got out and opened the panel door behind me. He reached forward, grabbed the green man by the collar and pulled him out. As he slid past me, I steadied his arm to help him down and out of the van.

Finding himself in the grip of one of the masked men was enough to put him over the edge. He immediately doubled over and heaved what was apparently a very large, chunky breakfast all over the ground. The man in the balaclava deftly jumped back and managed to avoid spillage on his shoes.

He yelled a few choice words, then shoved the poor sick man back into the van and slammed the door. As he was opening the door to get back into the driver's seat, I said to the man with the shotgun, 'You should get this poor fella a cuppa tea.'

He turned to me, the metal barrels pointed right at my face. 'Wha'?'

'He's just been sick and he's in a sweat. He needs a cuppa tea.'

Spittle came spewing out of the mouth opening of the balaclava. 'A cuppa tea? Am I a fucking caterer?'

His friend was now sitting next to him. He turned towards his partner in arms. 'What is it now?'

'This one thinks we should get the sicko a fucking cup of tea.'

The one who had nearly been thrown-up on waved his hand. 'Shoot her.'

I don't know who was more surprised – me, or the fella with the gun.

'I'm not gonna shoot her!'

His friend gave him what I can only assume was a terrifying glare – it was hard to tell with all the balaclavas.

'Well, not yet. Not for that.' His shotgun wobbled a bit. 'Not till I get orders to shoot someone.'

His friend slammed his hands on the steering-wheel. 'We should shoot the whole fucking lot of them and get the hell outta here.'

Several of the hostages gasped – or sobbed – and the man with the shotgun remained silent.

The sick man hung his head between his knees and moaned.

'How about a glass of water?' I asked, in a small voice.

'SHUDDUP!' That came from the two of them at once. I sat back and kept quiet.

Hours went by, and the robbers kept shifting around. The one who seemed to be the driver would run back into the store and consult with the third, and the one with the shotgun would occasionally get out and patrol around the van – but was never more than a step or two away from us.

Once, when he was outside the van, two of the hostages started whispering.

'I need to go to the toilet.'

'Oh, God, me too. I'm about to burst.'

I wished they hadn't said anything. Now all I could think about was my own bladder.

When Shotgun Man got back into the van, there was still some whispering going on.

He didn't even look back towards us, just waved his gun and shouted, 'Shuddup!' It had become a reflex.

I decided to speak up. Or perhaps my bladder prompted me. 'Any chance we could get a toilet break?'

He turned this time. 'What did I just say? I said SHUDDUP.'

'Okay, okay. It just may get messy back here.'

The two barrels moved very close to my face.

'No. One pull of the trigger and THIS will get very messy.'

'All right, all right.' I sat back. 'It just seems like you fellas have the winning hand, so I don't see what's taking so long.'

'What the hell are you talking about?'

'Well, you boys have the money, right?'

'Yeah, what if we do?'

'And you have hostages – whom you haven't hurt at all.'

'Yet,' he said. Rather grimly, I thought.

'Well, what have the coppers got on ya, then? You give back the money, turn us over safe and sound, and all they have ya for is attempted robbery. Easy as pie.'

Just then the driver's door opened and we were joined by our other captor. 'What's all this yapping? Tell them to shut their cake-holes.'

The barrel of the gun wagged a bit in my direction. 'She says we have the winning hand here.'

That made the driver turn around. 'Who is "she"?'

The barrel pointed at me again.

The driver gave me a brief look, then turned away. 'Ah, she's full of shit. Shoot her.'

'I'm not gonna fucking shoot her. Yet. She has a point – we give back the money and the hostages and no harm done.'

The driver rounded on him. 'NO HARM DONE? We fucking went in there with a shotgun and TOOK THEIR MONEY.'

'But you could give it back,' I interjected. 'The money hasn't left the premises yet.'

The driver reached over and made a grab for the shotgun. 'Give me that thing and *I'll* fucking shoot her.'

Fortunately, his friend was not about to give up his grip. He wrestled it out of the driver's reach. 'Stop that, ya gobshite. Think about it. So far, it's just *attempted* robbery.'

'That's a big difference in the eyes of the law,' I couldn't help adding.

'SHUDDUP!' They were getting quite practised at shouting together.

One of the other hostages nudged me with his foot. When I turned to look at him he shook his head at me. From further away I heard some soft sobbing and then a trickling sound. A small ribbon of liquid came rolling down the floor.

First vomit, now this. I was afraid of what might be next.

'I'm just saying,' said Shotgun Man, 'we don't hurt nobody, we don't take no money – we do very little time. 'Cause I ain't seeing no way outta this.'

'How do we know they won't throw us in jail and let us rot?'

'You just need a good barrister,' I piped up. 'I know a fella at Four Courts – he'd take good care of you.'

Shotgun Man looked at me. 'Yeah? Do you have his number or –'

'SHUDDUP!'

All on his own, the driver managed to scream so loudly I thought the windscreen would shatter.

'Jesus, all right.' Then Shotgun Man paused a moment. 'What's that smell?'

It was a total of six hours before the third robber came back to the van – followed by a slew of men in uniform. That is definitely the happiest I have ever been to see policemen. Though I know it had nothing to do with me, the boys did make the right decision – surrounded, and without any hope of a clean escape, they finally offered to return the money and release the hostages.

After being interrogated by the police and tended by some medics (mostly they just had to do some rather unpleasant cleaning), we were allowed to exit from the front of the store. As we headed out, huddled together, a barrage of lights and popping noises rose up in front of us. There were vans and cameras and microphones – a real bloody paparazzi mess.

Some fella with a microphone came up and stuck it in the faces of the first few hostages as they headed towards friends or loved ones who were welcoming them with screams and cries. Each one told him, in one way or another, to bugger off. Everyone was exhausted and just wanted to get home. No one wanted to talk about it. As everyone streamed away, I saw Tess and Doris waving at me and shouting. As I headed towards them, the man with the microphone edged up to me. 'Have you got anything to say about the experience? It must have been quite an ordeal.'

I blinked at him. 'Yes, yes – it's been a long day.'

'I know – but it would be great if one of you could talk to us for the television. Everyone else has said no. Please?'

I saw a man with a camera and another guy with a light creeping up behind him. I sighed. 'Sure enough.' I smiled at the camera.

Behind it, I saw Doris throw up her hands first in desperation and then in some hand gestures that were not at all ladylike.

20

Ah, you see. Here we are back to Doris again. Always there for me.

In the days after she died, I would close my eyes sometimes and try to picture the really big, really momentous, really outrageous, really terrifying or just really hilarious times in my life – and always Doris was there. Always. And opening them again, and seeing life carrying on without her there to share it with me, I saw an emptier place than I'd ever imagined or ever wanted to inhabit.

I tried getting out of the house at night. That helped a bit. I would go wherever there was some music on and sit through an evening of songs and chatting. Mind you, among the gang of us, there was no escaping the empty place where Doris had been. I knew they all felt it keenly as well. But it was also understood that we could not wallow in our loss, that we had to consecrate her death with the perseverance of life. So the singing was perhaps a bit more exuberant than before. The laughter more sharply edged. The conversation more fervent. I never forgot for a moment how much I was missing her, but the edge of my pain was dulled.

And it was there, among my friends, that I found my salvation and my damnation. I discovered drink.

Now, I had always enjoyed a jar or two when I was out

and about, just like everyone did. The thing that made this different was that before I had never *needed* to drink. I had indulged many times in beer and wine – and, of course, my exploits with *poitín* were legendary – but I had always been able to take it or leave it. I had never thought of it as a place to hide. But one night, when my heart felt like a stone, someone introduced me to brandy. And in its warm fire I found that I could finally drink enough to shut up the demons in my head. I could crawl into a dark, empty place and find, if not sleep, an unconsciousness that at least allowed me to rest.

At first, it was only occasionally – just on those nights when I knew I was approaching a meltdown – that I drank myself into a tipsy, mindless state. Everything would get pleasantly fuzzy and the jagged edges of my memories were blunted. It was just enough that I could still manage to get myself home, collapse onto my bed and remain blissfully semi-conscious until I had to get up and get the kids sorted. I convinced myself that they never noticed if I was a little the worse for wear.

But obviously I couldn't go out every night. And eventually just escaping on those nights when I could get away was not enough. I had to find a way to kill the pain on the nights when I stayed at home. And that was when brandy came home with me so that I could crawl inside it every night.

I developed a new routine. At the end of the long day, after I'd got kids and husband sorted, I would turn down all of the lights in the house except one in the kitchen. I would switch on the radio or the television, sit in my comfortable chair and start sipping my brandy. At first, I would sit and sip until I felt the heavy claws of pain stop raking across my heart. Then, as soon as I felt that I could slip into a pain-free haze, I would shift myself up the stairs and into my bed.

But as time went on sipping a glass or two until the pain was dulled was not enough. It needed to be erased. It needed to be expunged. So the drinking would go on until I was unconscious, right there in my chair. And for a good while I was able to wake myself up before the children came down so that they didn't know I'd never made it to bed. But eventually there came those mornings when they would find me, sloppily snoring in the chair, still in my clothes from the day before.

I don't know how long this could have gone on. If everything hadn't gone to Hell, perhaps I would still be drinking myself senseless today – because, God knows, I miss Doris now as much as I did back then. I wasn't really living: I was surviving by day, and killing myself by night. I convinced myself that I was coping and that no one was suffering. But God and His angels knew that I was crawling into a pit that would swallow me whole. So they sent me a message.

Going out for the music and the fun was leading to more and more unhappy results. There were mornings when I couldn't remember what I had done the night before. When my friends told me, it was funny – or embarrassing. Then there started to be the mornings when I couldn't remember coming home. I couldn't remember driving. I couldn't remember coming through the door.

Eventually there were those mornings when I awoke to discover I hadn't made it to my bed, just come in the door and collapsed on the sofa. Or the floor.

Eventually came the morning when I nearly died.

I still don't know what was different about that night – who I was with, how much I drank, why I was so out of my mind. But I drove myself home, and that thought frightens me to this day. The state I must have been in.

I awoke bleary-eyed, cramped, cold, and with a mouth that tasted like I had swallowed an old pair of socks. As I looked around, I couldn't believe it. It was in the early stages of daylight – and I was curled up in the grass in front of my doorstep. My car was next to me, the driver's door still ajar.

I began to panic. Had I hit something? I could have hit all kinds of things on my way – had I hit a tree? Had I hit another car? My God, had I hit a person? A child? I started to feel sick. I couldn't remember anything about driving home. Nothing.

It was difficult to stand up straight, but I managed to clamber up and inspect the car. There wasn't a mark on it that I could see. The keys were still in the ignition. But my clothes felt strange, damp and clingy, as if I'd been caught in the rain.

I checked myself in a clumsy, half-drunken attempt to see what was what. I was a mess. I had vomited on myself. And I had wet myself, too.

I sat down on the step, then bent over and gave in to a choking, gasping sob. I allowed myself to cry, letting go of all the bruising sorrow I had been holding back for so long, letting loose the flood of tears I had been trying to dam with alcohol.

I spent a few moments gathering myself, then grabbed my keys and let myself into the house. Keeping as quiet as I could, I took a shower in water as hot as I could stand. Then I came downstairs and made a pot of coffee. I drank the lot, one mug at a time. When I started to retch, I poured myself another mug and made myself drink it.

Still as quiet as I could be, I got back into the car and drove. I knew exactly where I needed to go.

I arrived at Mount Argus just as the morning traffic was getting into full swing. I didn't even think about it: Mount Argus was where you went if you had a problem like mine. The doors to the church weren't open, so I went to the reception desk at the monastery and told the brother there that I wanted to take the Pledge.

He didn't even blink, just looked me in the eye, nodded, and took me into a small waiting room. A priest came in. We talked for a few minutes – I gave him a brief summary of what I had been through and what I had done – and then, with a rosary in one hand and the other on the Bible, I took the Pledge: I swore to God and Heaven and all the angels and anyone else who might be listening that I would never drink another drop of alcohol for the rest of my life.

The priest was a kindly old man. He took my hand when we were done and said, 'You do know that this is just the start. Now you need to heal the wound that made you drink in the first place.' He handed me a card – it was for a psychiatric counsellor.

I took the card, fully intending to throw it away. In all

my life to that point I had never had a good opinion of counsellors, psychologists, therapists or any analyst who wanted to get inside somebody's head. I had known people who had gone through various types of therapy and spent years sitting on someone's couch yarning on and on about their childhood. I thought it was a load of worthless shite.

But that night the longing for the drink was like a burning oil on my soul. When the following morning finally came, I knew I wasn't going to be able to keep my Pledge without some help. So I called the lady whose name was on the card. Ruth.

To be honest, the first few meetings were just as painful as not drinking. I was beginning to despair that it was ever going to be worthwhile, and every day I was in agony, not knowing which was more terrifying: having another drink, or never having one ever again. I don't know exactly what the breakthrough was, but somehow Ruth prised something open and all of the pain I had been forcing out of sight broke free and slapped me right in the face. I thought I had been broken by grief, but at that moment I realized that I had been destroyed by my refusal to face it – that I needed to learn to live with my broken heart and stop retreating from it. There was nowhere to hide that would ever be safe. There was nothing in the bottle that would ever save me, that would ever be my friend, that would ever bring any kind of help or healing. I would have to find all of those things within myself.

In short, Ruth made me face my loss – and she saved my life.

Some day it will be my turn to pass over to the other side. I know Doris will be there waiting for me. And I still say that the first thing I will do is box her ears for putting me through all of this. God love her. Meanwhile I don't have the time to wallow in it.

21

In 2010, things were changing in my neighbourhood. There had been a large house nearby – well, two terrace houses that had been joined together, actually. It had been the home of an order of nuns for many years. I'd had my run-ins with nuns in the past, but this group were truly nice people and a blessing to the neighbourhood. Unfortunately, there weren't enough of them to justify such a large place so they had been moved elsewhere.

When the house became available, those of us who lived in the area were stunned to find out that the town council wanted to make it into a group home for drug and alcohol addicts. This house is very near the primary school – many kids walk past it twice every day.

I think it can be fairly said that I am a person who believes that everyone is entitled to a chance in life – and a second and third chance, if need be – so I didn't have a bit of a problem with the idea of a home for these people. But I did have a problem, along with my neighbours, with this particular home being in this particular area.

Why?

We were informed that it wasn't going to be a 'dry' house where the intention is to ensure that everyone is trying to stay sober. In a 'dry' house, if a resident shows up drunk or high, they aren't allowed to stay there. But in a 'wet' house, which was the kind they were planning to install in the former nuns' home, no effort is made to keep track of whether people are 'using' or not. Recovery from their addictions is left up to the individuals. That was problem number one for me.

And problem number two was the issue of where these people who were going to be living in the house had come from. Given the high rate of substance abuse in our area, I had no doubt that some of its inhabitants would be related to families nearby. I just couldn't believe that it would be suitable for little Johnny or little Sally to be walking to or from school and see their own ma or da sitting outside the house that everyone knew was for people with 'problems'. It was too close to home in just too many ways.

The more my neighbours and I got together and talked about it, the more determined we all were to get the thing nipped in the bud. Eventually one of my neighbours, a young fella named Jonathan, and I were holding regular meetings in my kitchen, and everyone who was interested was welcome. We called ourselves the Liscairne Action Group. We knew there was no point in just trotting over to the council and telling them to put a stop to it without offering any alternatives so we spent a lot of time researching and planning other ways to house and care for addicts. We also organized some protests and events to focus attention on what we were trying to do. We made posters and placards, marched in the streets and stopped traffic – literally – just to get the word out.

One evening, after one of our meetings, Jonathan and I were musing as to whether or not we could get any TDs to take up our cause. I knew of one politician who might be a good choice.

Frances Fitzgerald had already been a TD, a member of Dáil Éireann, for Dublin South-east and was currently a member of the Seanad, the upper house of Dáil Éireann. She had her eye on running for TD again, this time for Dublin Mid-west. I knew a bit about her – she was a former social worker and an activist for children and families. I told Jonathan I thought she might be someone with clout who would take our part.

Without much more discussion, at ten o'clock in the evening, we went through the phone book and found what we thought might be her home number, based on what we knew about the area she lived in. She answered the phone herself.

I didn't waste any time but got right to the point about what we were doing, and fortunately the small bit of press that our marching had attracted meant that she was aware of the situation. I had my ducks in a row and explained to her exactly what we were doing and why we were doing it. I made her aware that we were not a heartless, defensive group of snobs – and that, in fact, we had been doing some research into finding other locations and housing facilities that would be better suited to the folks in question. All of us in our action group felt that these people needed help, and deserved it. We just didn't think our family neighbourhood was the right place to offer it.

Frances listened – and also asked a lot of questions. Before I hung up that night, she had agreed to help us. Democracy in action!

She was as good as her word. Not only did she come along to meetings with us, she also got right out there and marched with us. Having her carrying around a placard called some attention to us – the press were very interested in what she had to say. The increased publicity we got by having her involved was a big boost, and other neighbourhood groups, similar to our own, from all over Ireland, who were having to fight to keep such homes out of family areas, contacted us.

Someone asked the council why a working-class neighbourhood such as ours (and all of the others, for that matter) had been targeted instead of a more affluent area.

The answer?

Because they thought that in a neighbourhood such as ours they would encounter the 'least resistance'. I'm not going to gloat about how wrong they were. Well, not much anyway.

We attended as many of the town-council meetings in Clondalkin as we could and took an active part in the discussions. Frances was always there for us. As I said, we had been doing some research into housing schemes for addicts that had worked well in other communities and we wanted these other options to be explored. But the whole scheme was like a giant box of shifting sand. Just when we thought we had pinned down one problem and a possible solution, we were informed that the 'problem' had been redefined. The proposed group home became less about addicts and more about homeless people. The language we were hearing at the meetings became more and more about 'getting people off the streets'.

If that was meant to defuse the situation, it was a horrible miscalculation. I know a thing or two about homeless people, and putting them into a group home with a load of folks who might have substance-abuse problems is about the worst way I can think of to help. Jonathan and I went out and looked at places that had been developed elsewhere, where apartment blocks had been converted into flats for the homeless and the results had been stellar. Many of those people have no interest in alcohol or drugs: they have simply hit a low point in their lives that far surpasses the low points most of us reach. They have lost everything. Absolutely everything. To get a job, they need an address. To get off the streets, they don't need to be dumped in a group setting with people who would only drag them back.

I spoke out at those council meetings and explained this as best I could. I didn't overwhelm the members with detail, but I did tell them a bit about all the fostering (for lack of a better word) I had been doing for most of my life. And, of particular importance, I knew that a lot of the people living rough on the streets of Dublin at that time had once been in foster care. It was a real problem with the system that those people, at the age of eighteen, had been deprived of the Social Services and foster care they had grown up with. Boom. You hit eighteen and you were done. No more foster home. You could get assistance to go to university or into vocational training. Other than that, you were on your own.

Now I kept many kids well beyond the age of eighteen if they weren't ready to go. I got no financial help from

Social Services for them but, then, I had spent most of my life taking care of kids out of my own pocket. But many other foster parents couldn't do that. And kids who weren't ready for college or training – or suited to it – were left with nothing to do and nowhere to go. It wasn't a big step to end up on the streets. So for me the issue of home-lessness was rather personal.

At last, we were told that the final decision would be made at the council offices in Tallaght so a group of us gathered and headed down there. But those council meet-ings were not the same as they were in our town: they were snobby affairs, where those of us who were mere voters and taxpayers were required to sit in a balcony above the chamber. While council business was going on, those of us relegated to being observers were not permit-ted to talk or interfere in any way. At least they let Frances join in, so we knew we had an advocate.

You can imagine just how well it sat with me to be there and say nothing while they blathered on about the plans they had for (a) people living on the streets, for whom they had not the slightest clue about their real problems and needs, and (b) our neighbourhood, about which they seemed to be equally oblivious with regard to the nearby school and the number of children who would pass by the house. I thought I was going to swallow my teeth sitting there listening to it all.

Finally one notable started talking about what a great idea it was to get 'these people' into a group home and how the concept had been proven to be so 'effective'.

I couldn't stand it. Decorum be bolloxed.

I jumped up and yelled, 'That's a load of nonsense! Take a look at what they did in Tallaght, where they converted a block of apartments for homeless people! It's been a brilliant success.'

God, the looks on their faces down below! You'd have thought I'd leaned over the balcony and dumped a chamber pot on their heads (which sounds like a good idea, now I mention it).

There was a lot of furore and fussing and a 'sergeant-at-arms' was sent up to the balcony to tell me to sit down and shut up.

Fine. I didn't want to ruin things for our cause, so I sat down and promised to keep my mouth shut. Which I did. Right up until the time when the next gobshite said something idiotic.

I was on my feet again and giving them an earful. Well, what was the point of being there if we didn't express our opinions and voice our concerns?

They tossed me out into the hallway.

In the long run, our group managed to explain to the council something that had apparently escaped their attention: the nuns' house was wheelchair-friendly as the place had been occupied by many elderly nuns. A few alarms went off. Housing for special-needs families? That was something we could all support. So, the Liscairne Action Group was officially disbanded when the town council announced that they would not create a group home for addicts or homeless people or anyone else in that property.

It was a sweet victory. Frances and many others had

made huge contributions of time and shoe leather. In many ways, I felt Frances was a bit like me: when she saw a problem, she wanted to dive in and fix it. Unlike me, she was politically astute and not at all reckless. I got the sense that the combination of our different approaches to problem-solving might be a pretty powerful tool. It turned out that she was making some very serious plans about my future and I didn't even know it.

In August of that year, after our glorious victory, I was driving my van full of friends and children on our yearly expedition to Cahirciveen for the music festival. It was a long journey from Clondalkin to County Kerry, and the usual circus of trying to get clothes packed, children fed, dogs walked, fuel in the tank, regular potty breaks – well, it had just about done my head in. I was way behind schedule due to all of the dilly-dallying and was getting a bit hungry and tetchy as I sat behind the wheel.

My mobile phone rang. One of my youngsters answered it for me and put it on my hands-free speaker phone. It was a very nice-sounding young lady who talked a load of gobbledygook about Rehab, the Irish charity that helps special-needs people, Quinn Insurance and RTÉ television, and some big show that would be on in September. Something about the annual People of the Year Awards. Well, of course I'd heard of it. The show is on every year. What had it to do with me? I couldn't imagine why she was telling me all this.

Finally she announced, 'So you see, Mrs Hogarty, Frances Fitzgerald nominated you for an award and you'll be receiving it at this year's show in September.'

She might as well have said, 'The moon is made of green cheese and you have been elected Queen of the Mice,' for all the sense it made to me. I was at a junction where I knew I had to look for a tricky turn so I wasn't paying a great deal of attention to what she was saying.

'Sorry, love, what was that?'

'I said that Frances Fitzgerald nominated you and you will be getting an award for Mother of the Year.'

That was when I knew someone was winding me up. I didn't know who, but I really wasn't in the mood for it. 'Listen, dear,' I said, 'pull the other one – it's got jingle bells on it.' I hit the button to end the call.

She tried to ring back a couple of times over the next few days, but I just ignored her. It was the silliest thing I'd ever heard of and I was too busy to waste my time worrying about who thought it was a funny prank to play on me. I figured I'd get them back, though, once I'd found out who it was.

Fast forward a few weeks. I'm in a huge ballroom, full of glamorous, well-dressed people – some of whom are quite accomplished and even famous. I'm at a table with my family, and Frances herself is at my elbow. She really had nominated me, and I really had won the award. It had seemed unreal at the time, and was still unreal as I sat there watching it happen.

I had Hughie with me, my son Patrick, his wife and their two children, my daughter Gwen, her husband and their two children. And Gwen's daughter had *her* daughter, my first great-grandchild. And I had six of my foster children as well. And somehow, in some way, I knew Doris was there, too. Good thing: it was a big room.

As much as I might have whinged at the woman who first rang me about the award, the reality of it was very moving. They showed a little film about my life and kids, then called my name and I went up to the stage. Suddenly that distance from the table to the stage seemed very, very far.

I guess, in the scheme of things, the journey that led me to walk up those steps and onto the stage had been a very long one.

Life after the award was a bit of a whirlwind. Mind you, my life generally is a whirlwind, but this was a different sort. I was being interviewed for newspaper articles. I was being interviewed on television. Film crews were hanging around my kitchen filming me on a 'typical day'. I was amazed that the general public finds peeling potatoes to be quality entertainment, but there you are.

Almost everywhere I go now, people come up to me and ask me about my kids. Or they ask advice about their own kids. In particular, people ask me how they can become foster parents.

Thank goodness for that, because we need more good caring foster parents. We need many more. And the one piece of advice I always give is this: do it because you want to help the child. Not because you expect the child to think of you as their mother or father. Or to love you for the rest of their lives. They might never love you. But you have to do the very best you can for them at all times, no matter what. Very likely they will never think of you as a parent – most of those kids already have a mother or father somewhere, and part of your job is to make sure that they can keep a healthy relationship with them, as far as that is possible. Fostering is one of the few jobs where your ultimate goal is not to be needed any more. If you think fostering is about anything other than that, you're doing it for the wrong reasons.

The People of the Year Awards changed my life in a lot of ways. I'm more 'visible', I guess you could say. I'm known as an advocate for children's rights and I get to be involved in a lot of things in the public sector that relate to it. I get to give people advice.

And now I'm quite often asked my opinion about things. And people actually listen.

About bloody time!

Obviously I haven't told the stories of all one hundred and forty children here (my daughter Gwen reckons it's more like two hundred, if you counted every 'stray' I brought in). There are some who don't want their stories told. And others' stories simply can't be told. But I have shared with you many of the most important ones, the ones that hit me the hardest or the adventures that made me laugh the most.

I get asked a lot if my former kids keep in touch – if they still think of me as 'family'. Well, I don't know how they think of me, but I definitely do hear from most of them from time to time.

Lily is still living with me and is at university. Two of her sisters grew up to do very well – one is a solicitor, the other a social worker. Charlie is married, has three kids and lives not too far away; he still keeps in touch. Rose moved to New Zealand and became a successful intensive-care nurse. Her mother moved there to be with her. Jeannie went on to university and became quite the career woman. I've even heard from one of the French boys on occasion. Both of them are married – one lives in Portugal, the other in France. Trevor has grown up to become a fine young man; he has a great job in the city and a lovely girlfriend.

Sharon left my house one evening to go to a film with some friends – and didn't come back for two years. I tracked her down, of course: she had moved in with a boyfriend (that didn't last long). I let her know that I knew where she was – it didn't seem to matter to her. At the end of her two-year adventure she reappeared on my doorstep: she needed money. And then, after about six months, she was gone again. She did this back and forth for several years, before she finally decided to move to Canada to be with her mother. I can't even imagine what that reunion was like. The last I heard, Sharon was in Alaska. Chances are, if she really needs something some day and has nowhere else to turn, I'll hear from her again. That's generally the way it goes.

A couple of years ago I had a phone call in the middle of the night – from Australia. It was one of the lads from Finglas I had taken in for a few weeks. He had gone to Australia to find work, had spent all his money on drink and been arrested as a vagrant. Mine was the only phone number he had with him of someone he thought might help. He'd been carrying it around for years. I wired him enough money to get out of jail and contacted some friends of mine over there who got him sorted. Last I heard, he was still there, working, and had settled in well.

So, I hear from many of my 'kids' – and some of them I don't. And that's okay, because the whole point was to help them find their feet so that they could take care of themselves.

And Frances Fitzgerald did all right as well. In 2011, after being elected TD, she became a member of the cabinet: she was appointed the first Minister for Children. She is still a champion for children's rights – I imagine she always will be. She was instrumental in getting financial assistance for foster children until the age of twenty-three. I'd say the two of us have made quite a pair.

And the town council not only did not make the nuns' house into a group home, they split the place back into two separate houses. They are now occupied by some lovely families with special-needs children. They are a delight to have in our neighbourhood.

People often ask me what I am doing 'these days', as if I have retired or something. As a matter of fact, I still have five children living with me. There's Lily, of course, a young woman now, a set of twins I took in some time ago, another lad who had lived with me for a while, left, then come back – and a girl who is the daughter of one of my previous 'foster' kids.

No, I haven't told you their stories. Their stories are still going on, so to speak. Check back with me in a few years – and I'll fill you in.

Epilogue

On my seventy-sixth birthday, it was time to renew my driving licence.

Easy-peasy. I popped down, had the eye test and all the usual nonsense. Just as I thought everything had been finalized, the young man at the counter stopped me leaving. 'It says here that you also have an HGV licence.' He was peering at this information as if it was a mistake.

'That's right.'

He looked up at me. 'You can't be serious. You have an HGV licence?'

'I most certainly do, and I've had it for over forty years.'

He tapped something on his keyboard. 'Well, you can't be renewing that as well. You'll only be getting your motor vehicle licence today.'

What a load of utter rubbish.

Well, that was what I wanted to say.

Instead I tried to be calm. 'Why on earth can I not renew it?'

'Because you're seventy-six years old.'

'And what has that to bloody do with anything?'

He gave me a disbelieving look. 'You can't possibly be driving lorries at your age.'

God love him, a young fellow like him didn't know what he was dealing with.

'And I can't possibly be leaving here without that licence. Don't even try it.'

I won't flatter myself and even pretend to think that I was at all intimidating. But he could certainly tell I was stubborn.

'I'll have to get my supervisor.'

'Well, you just go and do that.' What did he think? That I would be afraid to talk to his boss?

A few minutes later he returned, boss in tow. 'Mrs Hogarty,' the supervisor started, 'we can't possibly let you renew your HGV licence at your age.'

'Listen here, I had to go to Belfast forty years ago to get that licence because none of you down here would give one to a woman.' People around us were listening in. Good. 'And I'll be damned if you lot are going to take it away from me now.'

'Mrs Hogarty, let's be realistic here. When was the last time you drove a forty-foot trailer?'

I didn't miss a beat. 'About three weeks ago.'

His face looked as if I'd slapped it with a cold wet rag.

I was not winding him up. I really had been driving a lorry – I'd been helping my brother with his stock down at his flower and nursery business.

The supervisor and I had a stare-off for a minute or so. He looked away and did some stuff on a computer. Finally he said, 'Well, if you want to renew the HGV licence you'll have to take the test.'

If the poor innocent man expected me to wilt and back off at the idea of being retested, he was in for a surprise. 'Fine.'

That flummoxed him. 'Fine?'

'Yes, fine, I'll take the test. Where do I go?'

It was an absolute delight to see his astonishment.

He turned back to the computer and scrutinized some things on the screen. 'If you can get over there before twelve, you can do it today.'

'Grand. Where do I go?'

By now, I think he was tired of the uppity old dear. At least he knew that if I went off to take the test, I'd be somebody else's problem. He gave me directions and I drove to the outskirts of West Dublin and the facility for HGV licence tests.

Now, I have never been one to slob around in tracksuit bottoms or even a comfy set of elasticized knitted slacks. When I go out, I look like I'm going out. Even if it's just to go to the shops or to argue with some booby-brained nincompoop, I dress to the nines. That day, I was wearing a calf-length brown dress with gold embroidery and a matching jacket, a long rope of pearls, and my hair was curled, set and pinned. It looked damned lovely.

So, with my matching handbag hanging off my arm, all five feet two of me marched into the HGV office and announced that I was there to take the test.

The young fella there gawped a bit, then grinned. 'We were told a seventy-six-year-old woman was coming in here to take the test. I guess that's you, is it?'

Rather than being annoyed, he seemed delighted. That was nice for a change.

By the time I was ready to get into the cab of the truck and start the test, a small group of people had gathered to see us off. Word had got out about the little old mad woman who was going to drive the lorry.

I did ask for one concession. 'Look, lads, I'm no spring chicken – not as nimble as I used to be. Can you just give us a hand up into the cab?'

A couple of young men jumped forward. 'Sure thing,' they said, and helped me climb up. It wasn't all age, of course – high heels and a lovely skirt were a bit constricting for cab climbing.

But I climbed in behind the wheel just fine, no doubt the best-groomed applicant they had ever had.

And off we went. The examiner said nothing but I detected a bit of a grin as I put the rig into gear and headed into the testing area. At first, everything was pretty easy-going.

Then we got to an area where he said, 'It gets narrow here. If you take it too tight or try to back up, you'll hit the barrier and that'll be an automatic fail.'

'Fair enough.' I took my time and breezed through it unscathed.

When we got back to the office, an even larger group was waiting than had been there to send us off. As we climbed out of the cab, the examiner gave the crowd a thumbs-up – I had passed – and there was a raucous round of applause.

One young woman yelled at me, 'Thanks, missus!'

I asked her what she was thanking me for.

'We all placed bets on how you'd do and you just won me some money!'

You've got to be joking.

Meanwhile, someone asked if I was 'that lady who's been on the telly'. No doubt bets had been placed on that as well. I answered, yes, I was that lady on TV – the one with all the kids. They were delighted with themselves for having recognized me. They then insisted on buying me a coffee. Coffee turned into lunch and I had to tell them loads of yarns about my years of driving lorries and raising kids. My half-hour trip to renew my licence had ended up taking half of the day.

With my HGV licence in hand, resisting the urge to go back to the supervisor and wave it under his nose, I got behind the wheel of my family mini-van and headed home.

I was a bit put out, to be honest. All the fuss at the HGV place had caught me off guard and I wasn't at all sure I was happy with all the attention – or with being recognized. Why could I never get through a normal, typical day like other people?

I blamed the People of the Year Awards and all the publicity that had come with it. The radio interviews, the newspaper articles, the television appearances – the general invasion of privacy. I was feeling quite sorry for myself, to be honest.

And then I couldn't help but imagine what Doris would have said.

She would have leaned over my shoulder and given me a big thump. 'Awards, my arse, Rio. Your life's always been like this. Nothing has ever been usual or normal or ordinary with you. It's always some kind of adventure or other, no matter what you do. Might as well stop blaming it on anything other than your own self. So now . . . what's next?'

I had to smile. Yes, indeed, I thought, as I headed home. What's next?